BELFAST

STREET ATLAS & GUIDE

We all like to kill two birds with one stone, so to speak, but the Belfast Street Atlas & Guide is that extremely rare bird which offers several different products for the price of one.

Firstly, it is a street atlas of the Belfast area, based on the Ordnance Survey. These maps, together with separate rail and bus maps, will help you to navigate your way through and around the city.

Secondly, it is a detailed guide to the best of what Belfast has to offer. Whether you are visiting for the first time or have lived here all your life, our aim is to help you make the most of this increasingly vibrant city as it reaps the dividends of the ongoing peace process.

The guide is written and published in Northern Ireland, and is based on contributions from people who have immersed themselves in Belfast's social scene with scant regard to their need of sleep or the health of their livers. Having said that, we are always keen to hear alternative views. If you have any recommendations to make or any contrary views to express regarding any of our choices, please write or e-mail to the addresses given on the page opposite. Any contributions which we use in the future will be acknowledged and a copy of the next edition will be sent in return for the best letters.

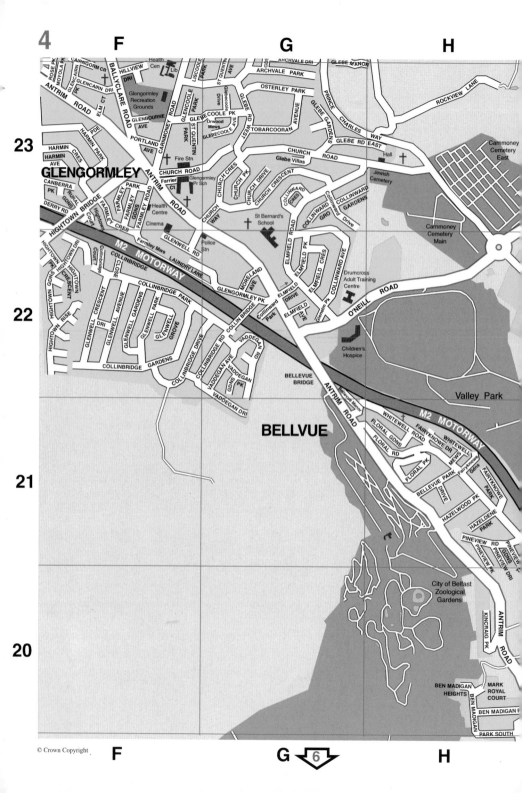

BELFAST

STREET & ATLAS GUIDE

CONTENTS

Scale of maps is 1:15,000 (4.2 inches to 1 mile)

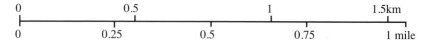

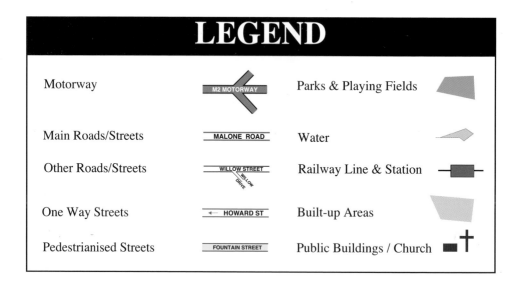

The maps on pages 4 to 28 are based upon the Ordnance Survey of Northern Ireland with the permission of the Controller of Her Majesty's Stationery Office. Crown Copyright reserved. Permit number 60295.

Printed by The Universities Press (Belfast) Ltd.

Edited by Paul Slevin. Comments, suggestions and inquiries should be addressed to him at the address below. Published by Causeway Press (N.I.), 17 Osborne Park, Bangor, N.Ireland BT20 3DJ. Phone 07768 172442. E-mail paulslevin@talk21.com

DISTRIBUTION: Distributed by Eason Wholesale Books.

ACKNOWLEDGEMENTS: Thanks go to Catherine Coyle, Gerri Slevin, Nell Slevin, Marianne Slevin, Vincent McGovern, Peter Welsh, Gordon Welsh, Chris McFerran and Barbara Mulqueen for their help and research.

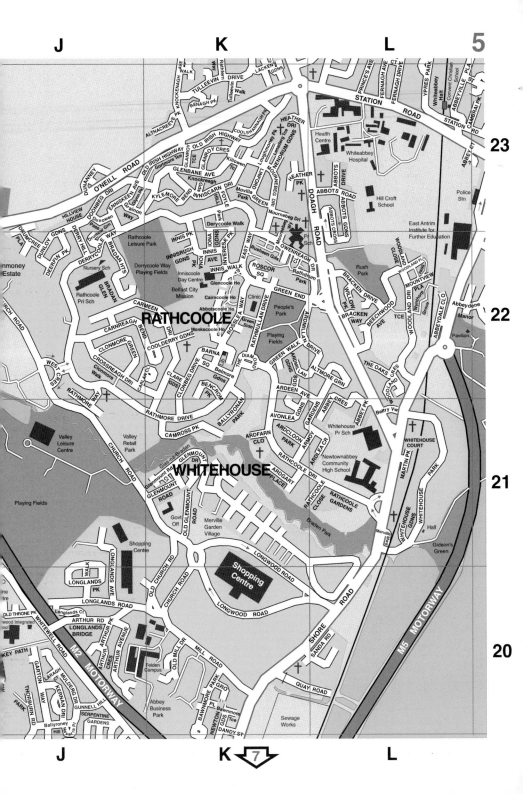

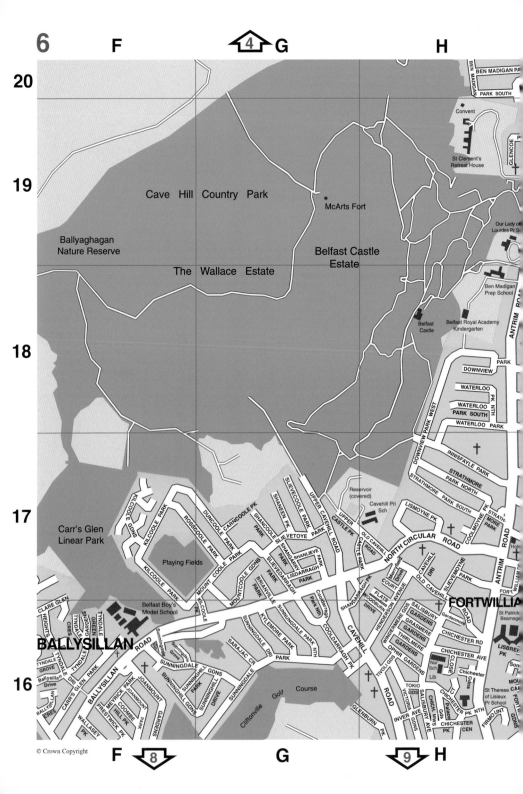

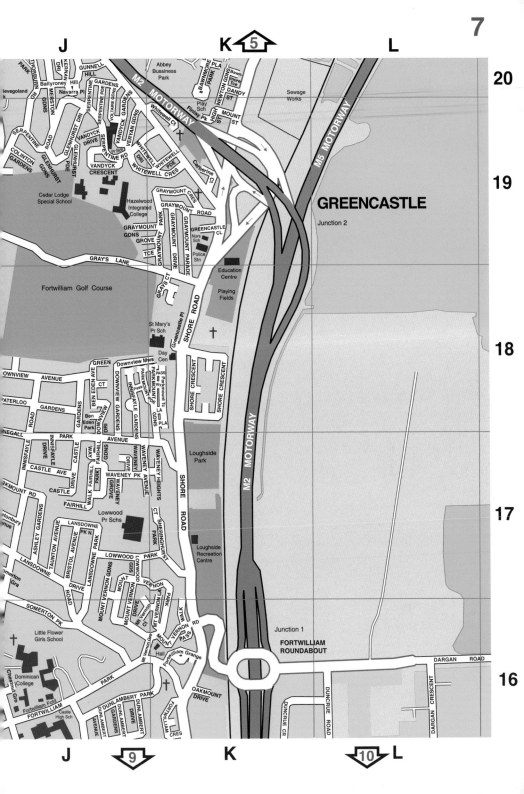

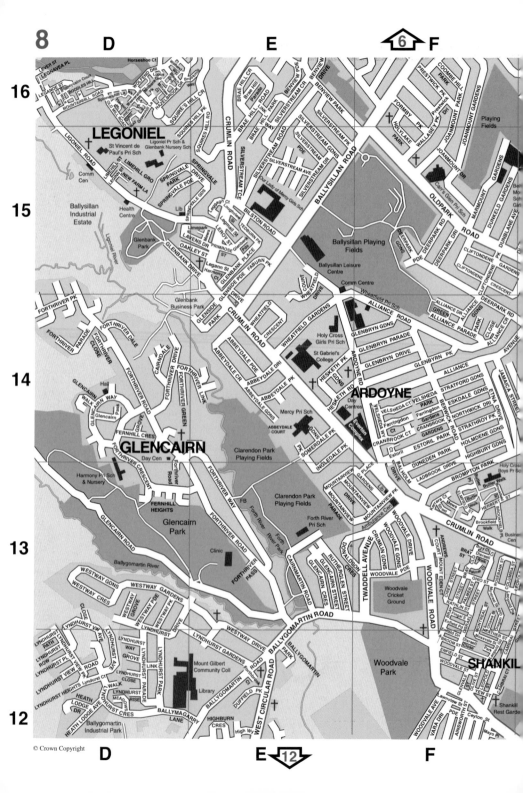

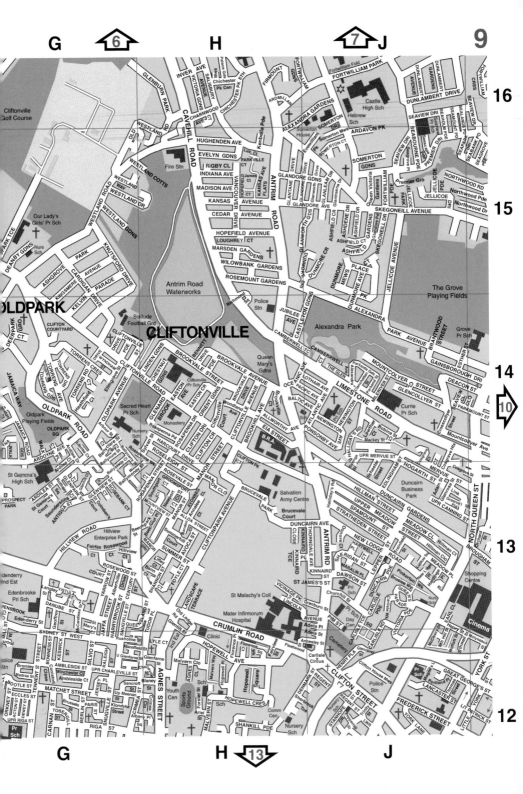

16

15

14

28

13

12

Heysham Ferry Terminal

Victoria Channel

WORKMAN ROAD

Belfast Dry Dock

Repair Quay

East Twin Island

EAST TWIN ROAD

WOLFF ROAD

MUSGRAVE CHANNEL RD

Musgrave Wharf

Musgrave Channel

Oil Berth 3

Oil Berth 2

Oil Berth 1

AIRPORT ROAD

AIRPORT ROAD

AIRPORT ROAD WEST

MOSCOW ROAD

HERON ROAD

DEPOT ROAD

George Best
Belfast City Airport

Terminal
Building

SYDENHAM BY-PASS

Blanchflower
Park

Playing Fields

Club
Houses

Aircraft Park

Alderman Tommy Patton
Memorial Park

HOLYWOOD ROAD

Ashfield Girls
High School

SYDENHAM

Victoria
Park

Boating Lake

Playing Fields

Bowling
Green

CONNSBANK RD

SYDENHAM BY-PASS

FB

INVERARY AVE

INVERARY DRIVE

INVERNOOK PARK

INVERNOOK DRIVE

INVERLEITH DR.

INVER CT.

INVERWOOD GDNS.

INVER CT.

Rockville
Ave.

Sydenham
Halt

VICTORIA DRIVE

VICTORIA DRIVE

VICTORIA ROAD

LARKFIELD DRIVE

LARKFIELD GDNS

LARKFIELD ROAD

Larkfield Manor

CONNSBROOK PARK

CONNSBROOK PK.

SANDBROOK PARK

Sydenham
Pr Sch

Victoria Pk
Halt

PARK AVE.

KYLE ST.

HILL'S AVE.

LISAVON DRI.

LISAVON ST.

GROVE

STRANDBURN ST.

STRANDBURN PARK

Larkfield Gro.

Larkfield Ct.

LARKFIELD
PARK

Strand Dri.

Wellwood Ave

St Mark's
C.E. Sch.

STREET

CONNSWALL AVENUE

VIDOR CT.

VIDOR GDNS

AVENIEL

PALMERSTON ROAD

STATION ROAD

DENORRATON PK.

Inverwood
Court

Inverwood
Mews

Tudor Dale Ct.

VICTORIA CT.

HOLYWOOD ROAD

CLONAVER PARK

CLONAVER DRIVE

CLONAVER
CRES. STH.

CLONAVER
CRES NTH.

OODMANOR
COURT

CAROLHILL
GDNS

CAROLHILL DRIVE

CAROLHILL PARK

ASHBROOK DR.

Ashfield
GDNS

HELGOR PK.

HELGOR PK MEWS

ARDVARNA
PK.

ARDVARNA
CRES

Ashford

NORWOOD CRES

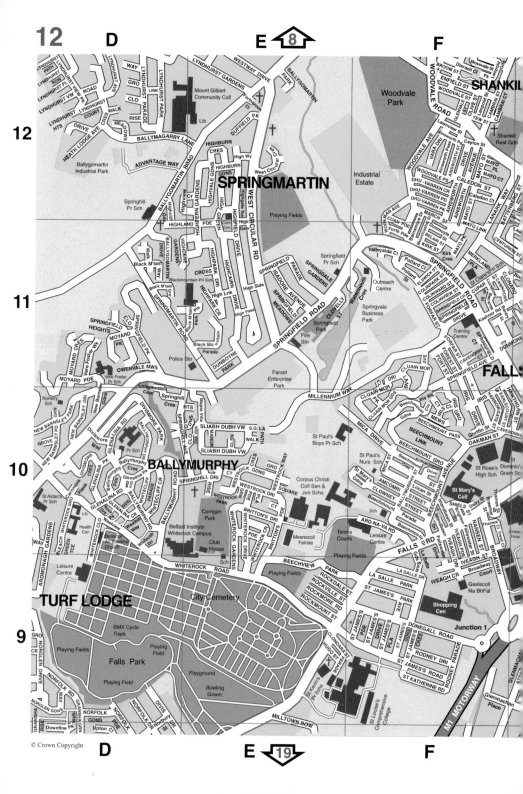

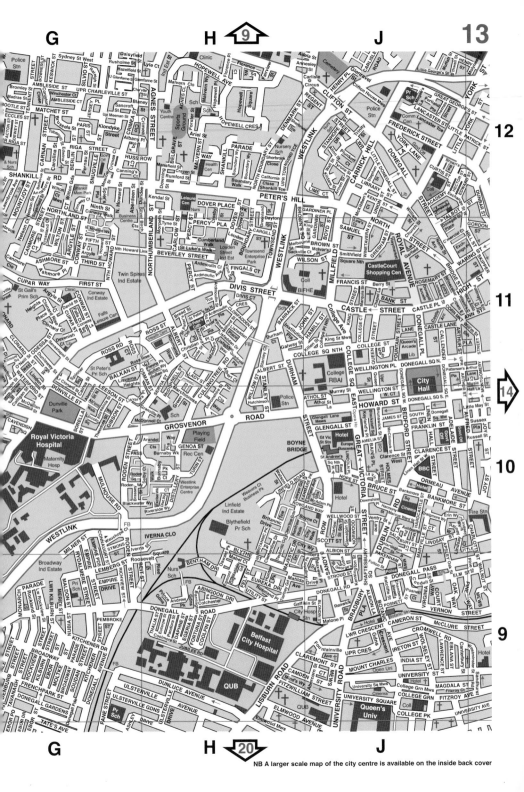

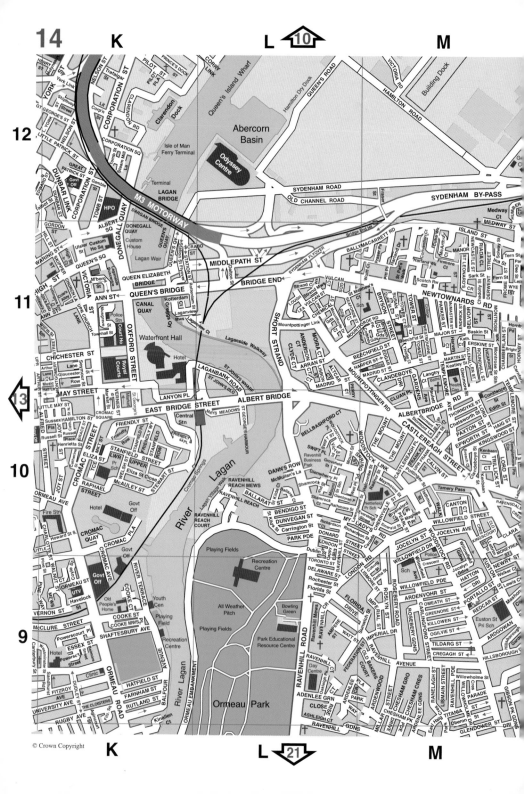

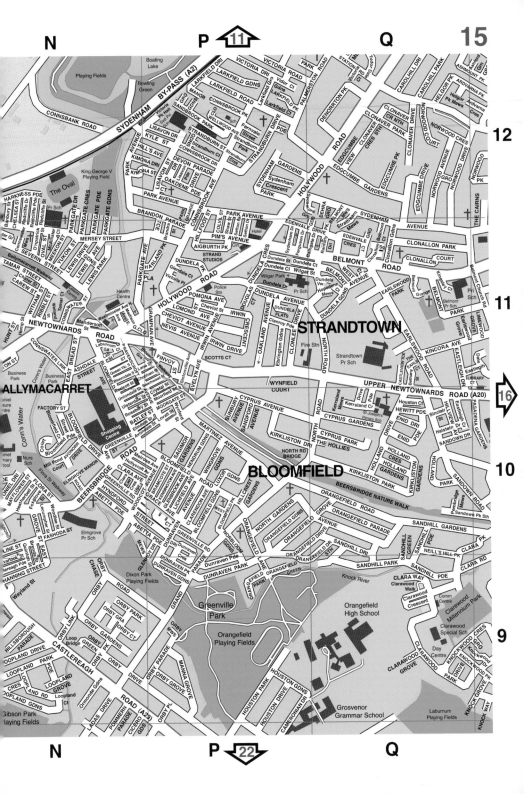

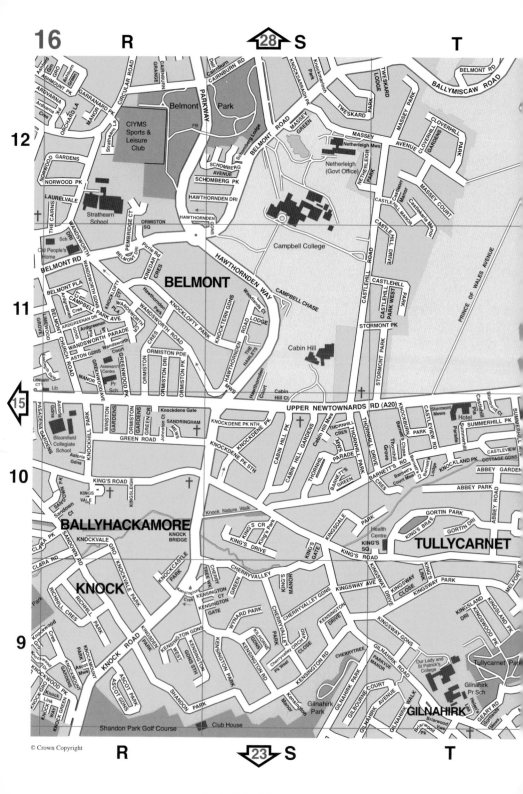

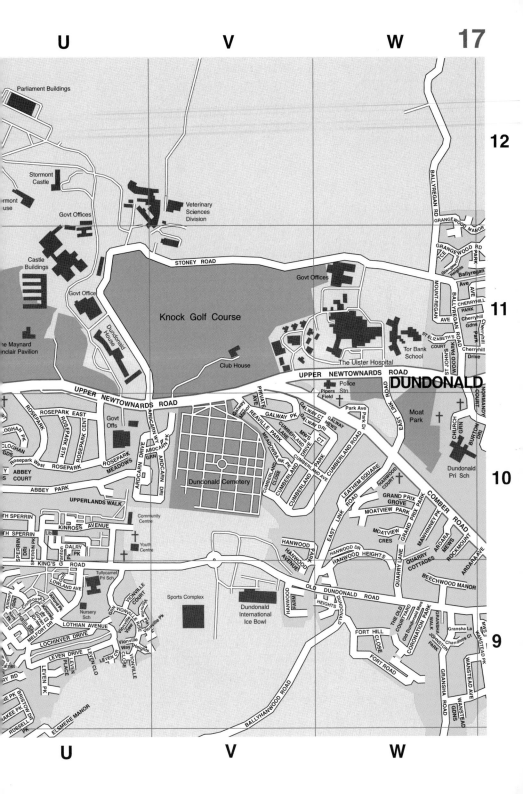

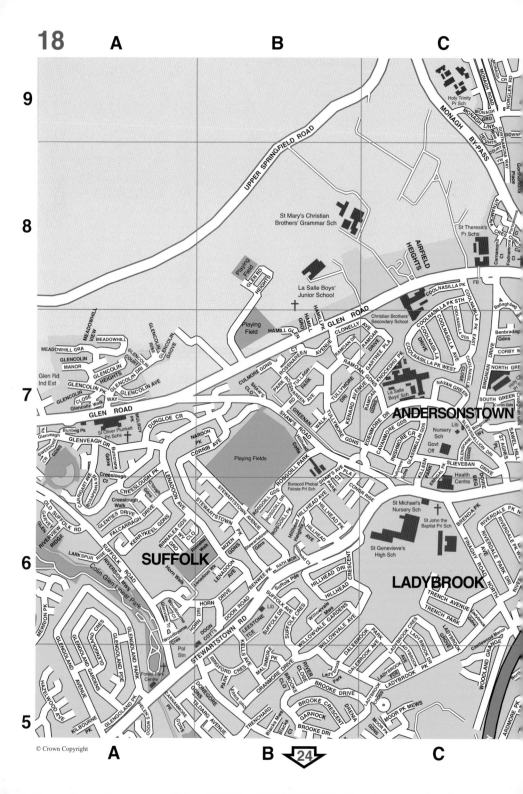

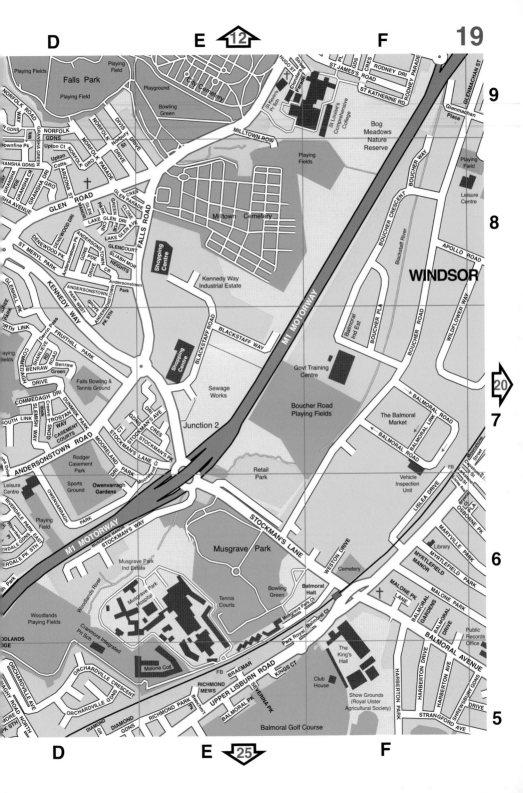

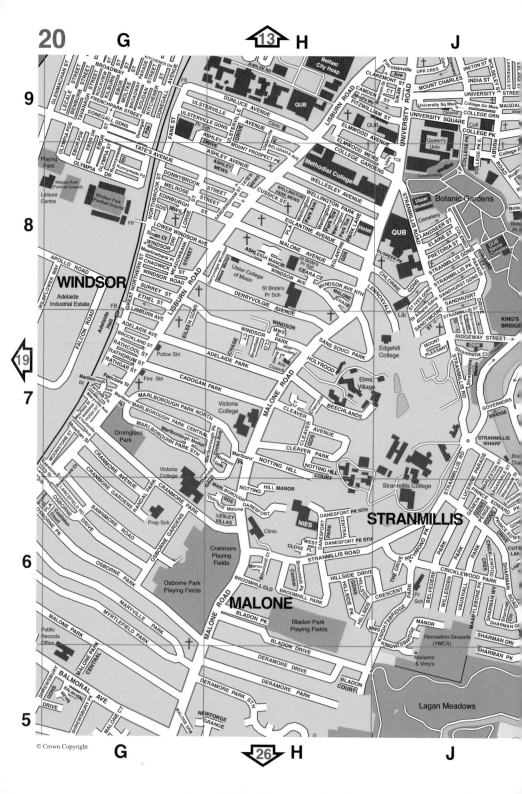

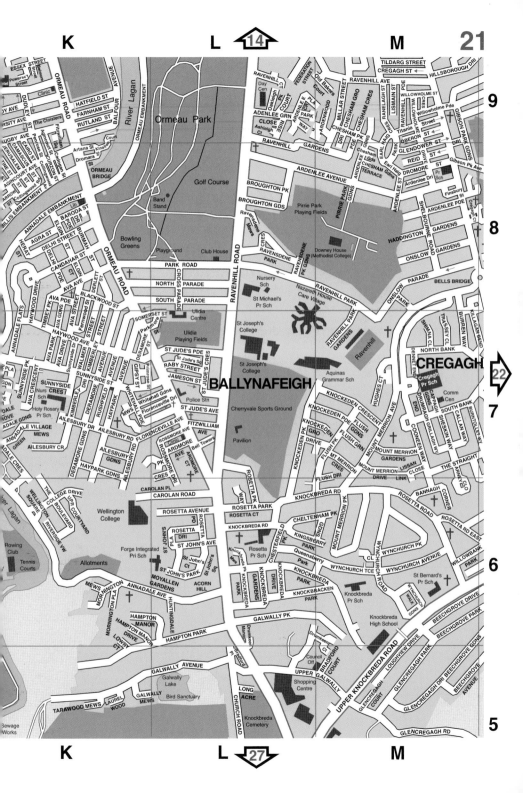

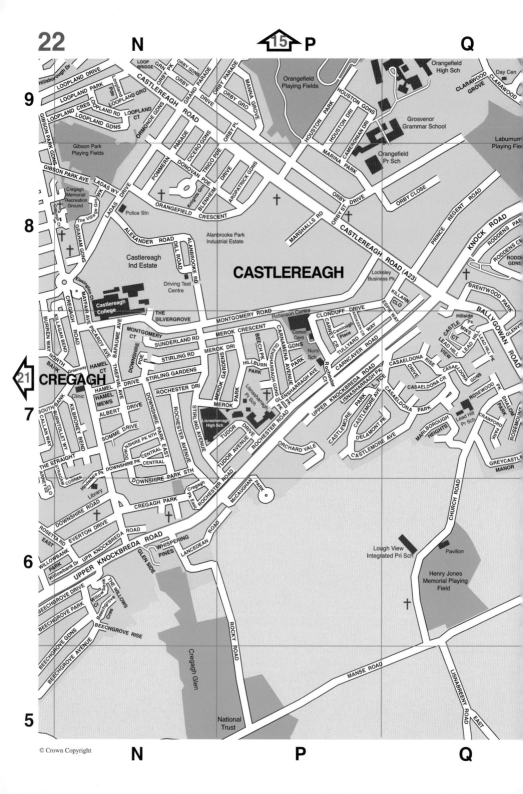

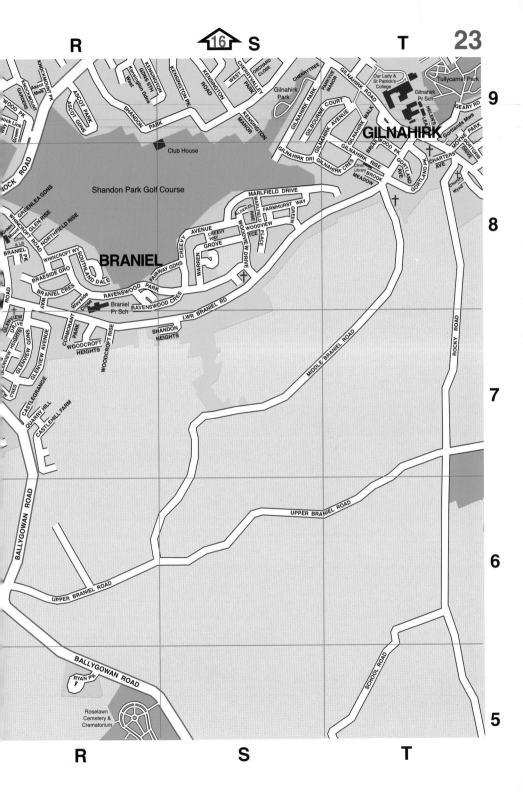

16

9

8

7

6

5

KNOCKMOUNT PK
Ascot Mws
KNOCKMOUNT PK
Ascot Mws
WOOD PK
GARDENS
Knock Link
Green
ASCOT PARK
ASCOT GDNS
KENSINGTON
GDNS STH
Kensington Gdns
West
KENSINGTON PK
KENSINGTON PARK
SHANDON PARK
WEST
PARK
CHERRY VALLEY
PARK
ORCHARD
CLOSE
CHERRYTREE
Gilnahirk
Park
GILNAHIRK PARK
GILBOURNE COURT
GILNAHIRK WALK
PARKVUE
MANOR
GILNAHIRK ROAD
Our Lady &
St Patrick's
College
Gilnahirk
Pr Sch
Tullycarnet Park
GEARY RD
GORTLAND PK
MOYNE PARK
MOYNE
DRIVE
Gortlends Mws
GILNAHIRK AVENUE

NOCK ROAD

KENSINGTON MANOR

Club House

Shandon Park Golf Course

GILNAHIRK

GILNAHIRK DRI
GILNAHIRK CRES
GILNAHIRK RISE
Clinic
Library
MEADOW
BRIARWOOD PK
GORTLAND AVE
GORTLAND PK
CHARTERS
AVE
ST HELENS
LEA
Church
Wynd

GREENLEA GDNS
GLEN RISE
NORTHFIELD RISE
WHINCROFT ROAD
Green
Mount
Eden
Clinic
& Lib
BRANIEL
PK
WHINCROFT WY
BRAESIDE GRO
SOUTHLAND DALE
BRANIEL CRES
AVE
ROAD
Wayside
Cross
Braniel
Pr Sch
RAVENSWOOD PARK
RAVENSWOOD CRES

MARLFIELD DRIVE
ALDER CL
MARLFIELD
RISE
FARMHURST WAY
MARLFIELD
PLACE
GREEN
CREEVY
AVENUE
CREEVY
WAY
WOODVIEW
TCE
WOODVIEW DRIVE
WARREN
GROVE
FAIRWAY GDNS

BRANIEL

LWR BRANIEL RD
SHANDON
HEIGHTS

GLENVIEW
DRIVE
GLENVIEW HEIGHTS
AVE
GLENVIEW GDNS
GLENVIEW AVENUE
CORMORANT
PARK
WOODCROFT
HEIGHTS
WOODCROFT RISE

CASTLEGRANGE
QUARRY HILL
CASTLEHILL FARM

BALLYGOWAN ROAD

MIDDLE BRANIEL ROAD

ROCKY ROAD

UPPER BRANIEL ROAD

UPPER BRANIEL ROAD

SCHOOL ROAD

BALLYGOWAN ROAD
RYAN PK

Roselawn
Cemetery &
Crematorium

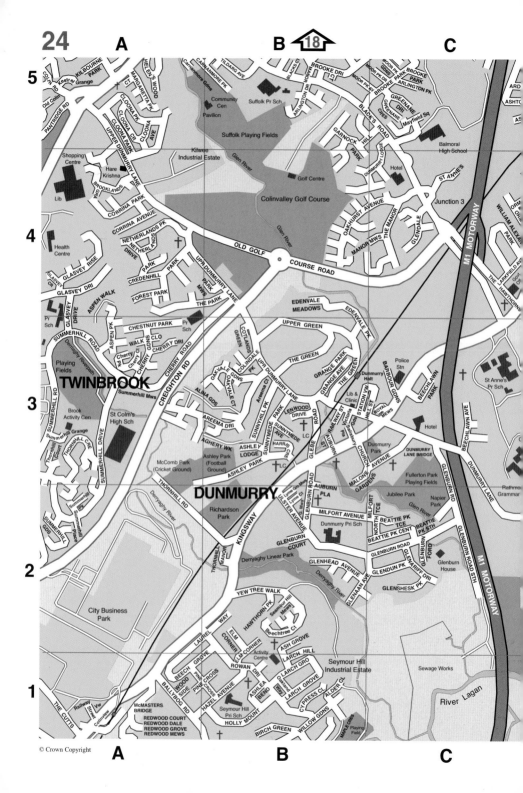

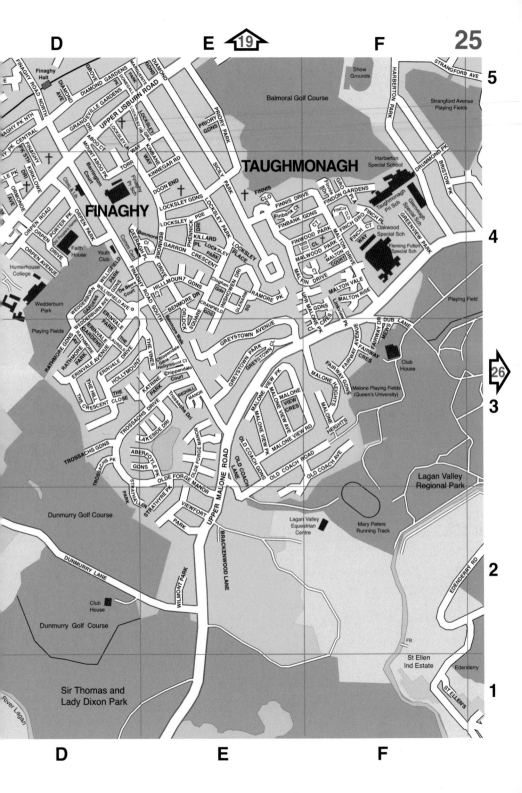

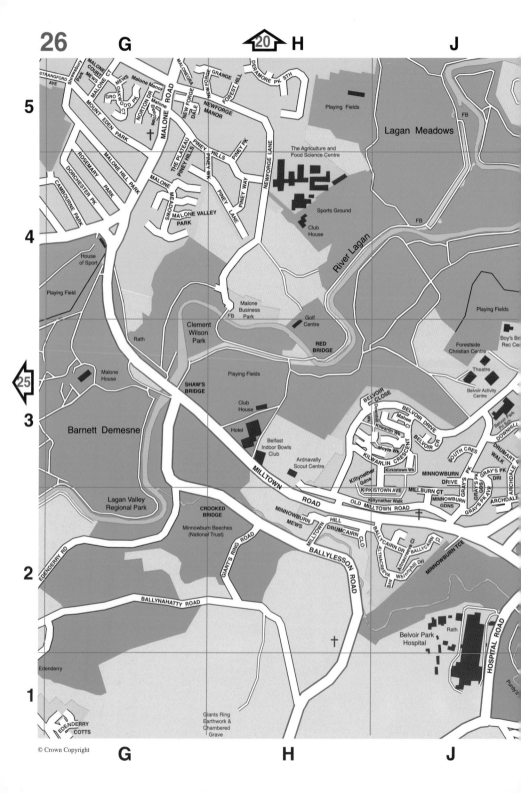

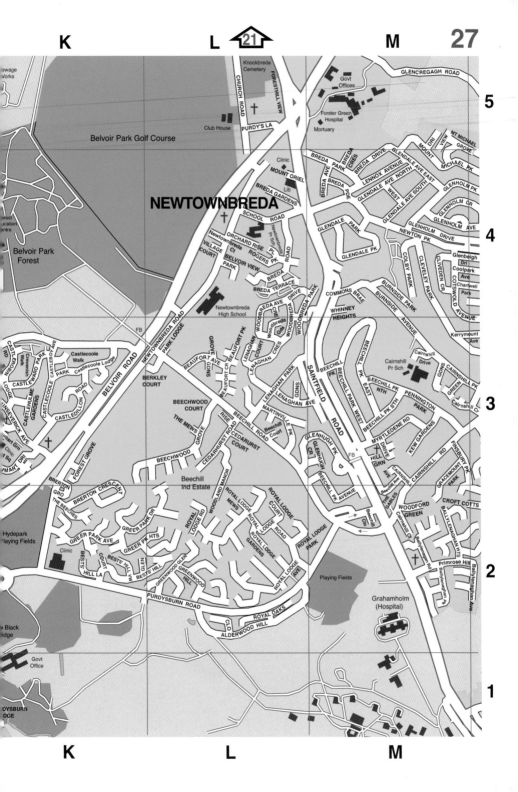

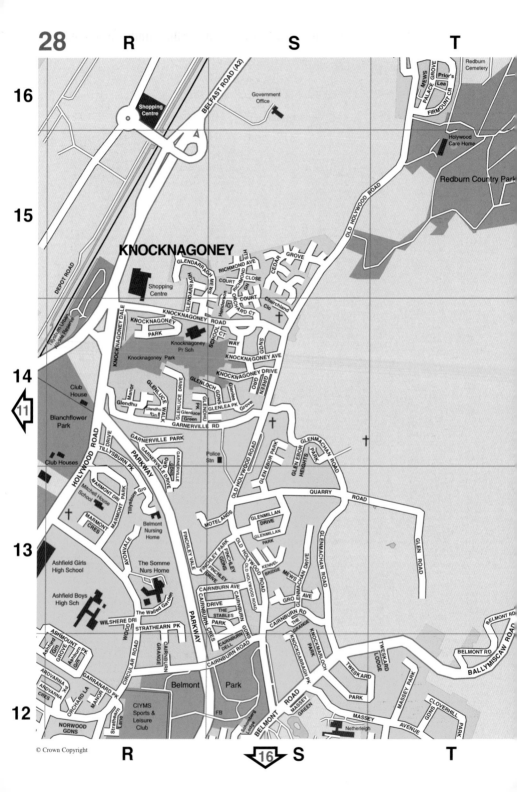

Due to insufficient space, some streets and/or their names have been omitted from the street map. Street names below which are prefixed by a * are not represented on the map, but they can be located by referring in the index to the name of the street which follows in brackets.

STREET INDEX

STREET INDEX

32

STREET INDEX

STREET INDEX

41

Belfast, like so many other cities, grew up on the banks of a river - its Irish name, *Béal Feirste*, means 'the mouth of the sandy ford'. It enjoys a beautiful setting on the shores of Belfast Lough, sheltered on one side by the mountains of Antrim and on the other by the green hills of County Down. The city itself fails to live up to the beauty of its setting, lacking the graciousness of Dublin, a reflection of the fact that Belfast's city fathers were Victorian industrialists rather than Anglo Irish aristocrats. Thirty years of 'troubles' have left their mark but the tide has turned in recent years, and Belfast is definitely on the up and up, with billions of pounds of investment helping to regenerate the city, most notably along the banks of the River Lagan.

Statue of Lord Carson in front of Parliament Buildings at Stormont

Belfast's native population was largely undisturbed by visitors until the Anglo Normans arrived in the 12th century. Its defences were strengthened with a castle built by the knight adventurer John de Courcy in 1177 but Norman power was eroded by an onslaught from the Gaelic clans, particularly the O'Neills of Clandeboye.

By 1542, Henry VIII had proclaimed himself King of Ireland as well as England, and the Reformation came to Ireland. In 1603 Sir Arthur Chichester was sent by James I to mastermind the Plantation of Ulster, which saw the arrival of thousands of Lowland Scots and the beginning of the Protestant Ascendancy. By 1613, King James had granted Belfast a charter of incorporation, which can still be seen today in the City Hall, and the town had taken its first step on the road to becoming a major city.

With Charles I beheaded and the English monarchy abolished, Oliver Cromwell landed in Ireland with a large army in 1649, ushering in a particularly bloody and savage era in Irish history. By the time the monarchy was restored in 1660, Belfast was a prosperous port, shipping produce from Plantation farms to Britain and abroad. English and Scottish settlers continued to flood in and the town's population was overwhelmingly Protestant at a time when Catholics made up most of the population of Ireland.

By 1688, Catholic King James II

had been deposed in favour of his daughter, Mary, who ruled jointly with her Protestant husband, William of Orange. Ireland was set to become a battlefield for a religious war involving most of Europe's major powers. In 1690 James lost the Battle of the Boyne to King William and this victory is still commemorated today by thousands of Ulster Orangemen with parades throughout Northern Ireland every year on the 12th of July. After defeat at the Battle of the Boyne, Catholics and other non-Anglicans suffered under the Penal Laws, Gaelic culture was driven underground, and the seeds were sewn for the struggle for Irish autonomy from England.

Implementation of the Penal Laws by the English forged an unlikely alliance between Belfast's middle class Presbyterians and Catholics, who together sought basic rights for all, and a transfer of power from the English ruling class. Inspired by the American War of Independence and stirrings of revolution in France, a group of merchants led by Henry Joy McCracken and the Dublin revolutionary, Wolfe Tone, founded the Society of United Irishmen in 1791. Their efforts to unite the people of Ireland against English Rule foundered with the failed 1798 Rebellion. Rebel leaders were hanged, the Irish Parliament in Dublin was abolished, and the Act of Union of 1801 brought Ireland into a United Kingdom with Britain, with the seat of political power in Ireland moving from

Dublin to Westminster.

A century of political turmoil followed. Daniel O'Connell helped to achieve Catholic emancipation in 1829 and, as Protestant influence weakened, sectarian tensions rose in Belfast and sporadic violence ensued. Economically, however, things were looking up. The Industrial Revolution saw Belfast grow into one of the world's major commercial ports. Belfast thrived on the development of its ship building and textile industries and, when Queen Victoria visited in 1888, she granted city status at a time when the population had grown to more than 300,000.

Political storm clouds continued to gather, however. The famine years of the 1840's had heightened anti British sentiment in Ireland, and an abortive rebellion by the Irish Republican Brotherhood in 1868 led to calls for Irish Home Rule. The case for Irish autonomy was taken up in the English parliament at Westminster by the Protestant leader Charles Stewart Parnell. Parnell died in 1891 and the political vacuum which resulted was eventually filled by a new breed of political nationalism with the establishment of Sinn Fein (Ourselves Alone), a political movement which advocated a boycott of the English parliament.

As momentum towards Home Rule increased, unionists in Ulster rallied to oppose it and made clear their willingness to use force if necessary.

Samson and Goliath at the shipyard

Belfast had prospered as part of the British Empire and unionists feared Catholic domination and economic decline in the event of an independent Ireland.

With Britain engaged in the First World War, the Irish Republican Brotherhood, often referred to as "the Fenians', organised the occupation of several strategic buildings around Dublin and declared an Irish republic from its headquarters in the General Post Office on Easter Monday 1916.

The Easter Rising was quashed after six days of fighting with British forces, who numbered 20,000 troops, and sixteen of the rebel leaders were later executed. Fourteen were shot in Kilmainham Gaol in Dublin. Sir Rodger Casement was hanged later in Pentonville Prison in London. Casement Park, home of the Antrim GAA teams in West Belfast, is named after him.

A wave of public sympathy resulted from the executions, and Sinn Fein secured an overwhelming victory in the 1918 elections.

A growing divergence between mainly Catholic nationalists and mainly Protestant unionists was highlighted by the fact that 5,500 men from the Ulster Division died for Britain during the Battle of the Somme, only months after the Easter Rising in Dublin. This helped to strengthen the already strong bonds between Britain and unionists in the north of Ireland,

and it was clear by that time that Ulster could not be forced into an independent Ireland.

A war of independence between British and Irish republican armies soon followed the 1918 elections and, after two years of fighting, the IRA general, Michael Collins, signed a treaty in 1921 which resulted in the creation of the Irish Free State, comprising 26 of Ireland's 32 counties. The other six counties became known as Northern Ireland and remained within the United Kingdom, although government powers were transferred from London to a new, unionist-dominated parliament, based at Stormont on the outskirts of Belfast. Collins said at the time that he was signing his own death warrant and he was proved right the following year.

The birth of Northern Ireland came at an inauspicious time. The Great Depression of the 1920's crippled the industries upon which Belfast had been built. The Second World War brought some respite with a sharp increase in ship and aircraft production, although the city suffered heavy bombing during the Blitz of 1941. The advent of the welfare state led to improvements in the quality of life for Belfast's citizens after the Second World War, but the concentration of power in the hands of unionists led to dissatisfaction among many Catholic nationalists who felt that they were being discriminated against when it came to jobs, housing and political power.

When the Civil Rights Association marched in Derry in 1968 demanding 'one man, one vote' in council elections, there were violent scenes. By August 1969 sectarian violence was flaring in Belfast and the British army was sent in to separate Catholic and Protestant communities. By 1972, the British government had dissolved the Northern Irish parliament at Stormont and power was transferred back to London. By this time the IRA had been reactivated and a nationalist campaign was under way to achieve British withdrawal from Northern Ireland.

Press and television conveyed pictures of Belfast as a war zone for the next twenty five years. Since the first

paramilitary ceasefires of 1994, however, the city has experienced a seachange in both atmosphere and environment. Physical barriers for the most part have been removed while work continues to bridge religious and political divisions. Life has returned to Stormont in fits and starts, with the establishment of a power sharing assembly, designed to fill a vacuum previously occupied by violence. Our politicians sit there occasionally when they are not in a huff with one another. Despite these birthing pains, times appear to have changed for the better and visitors are invariably impressed with the air of normality around Belfast these days.

Cultural life never disappeared, even during the worst years of the Troubles, but as people dedicate more of their energies to everyday leisure activities, the arts are raising their profile in the city. Leading lights include the Ulster Orchestra and its spectacular new home, Belfast's Waterfront Hall, the newly refurbished and extended Grand Opera House which plays host to many visiting international artists, the Lyric Theatre who nurtured the talents of Liam Neeson when he was still speaking with a Ballymena accent, and the Belfast Festival at Queen's which takes place every year in late October and early November.

When it boils down to it, however, its people are Belfast's greatest asset, even if they also represent its greatest liability! Like the harshness of the local accent, there is a bluntness associated with the local character - they tell it as they see it - but there is also warmth, friendliness and, above all, good humour, although it pays to recognise irony at fifty paces as most of Belfast's best one-liners are delivered with a straight face.

Whether it's novelty value, or simply a natural interest in people, especially people from farther afield, Belfast is particularly welcoming to tourists and visitors to the city. Whether you are living here or just passing through, the sections which follow try to point you in the right direction and aim to ensure that you make the best of all that Belfast has to offer.

AIR TRAVEL

Belfast International Airport

Known locally as Aldergrove, Belfast International is situated about 18 miles north-west of the city centre, off the M2 motorway (see map on inside front cover).

Airport Express 300, a 24 hour bus service to Belfast, leaves every 10 minutes from in front of the terminal building, less frequently during the night and at weekends. Buses stop in the city centre at Laganside Buscentre and at the Europa Buscentre which is adjacent to Great Victoria Street railway station, and the journey time is around 40 minutes. Tickets currently cost £6 for a single journey, or £9 return, and can be bought at the tourist information desk in arrivals or from the driver. For details of onward journeys by bus or train to other parts of Northern Ireland and to the Republic of Ireland see pages 46-49.

The airport's taxi rank is also in front of the terminal building and the journey to the centre of Belfast takes about 25 minutes and costs around £25. Most of the major car hire companies have reception desks in the arrivals concourse.

For further information and details of all flights from Belfast International Airport, phone (028) 9448 4848 or visit www.belfastairport.com. Airlines currently flying from the airport are listed below along with their destinations:

Bmibaby
www.bmibaby.com
Phone 0870 264 2229
Birmingham, Cardiff, Manchester, Nottingham East Midlands

Continental
www.continental.com/uk
Phone 0129 377 6464
New York Newark

easyJet
www.easyjet.com
Phone 0871 244 2366
Alicante, Amsterdam, Berlin

George Best Belfast City Airport is only two miles from the city centre

Schoenefeld, Bristol, Edinburgh, Faro, Geneva, Glasgow, Inverness, Krakow, Liverpool, London Gatwick, London Luton, London Stansted, Malaga, Newcastle, Nice, Palma, Paris Charles de Gaulle, Rome Ciampino

flyglobespan
www.flyglobespan.com
Phone 08705 561 522
Orlando Sandford, Toronto (Hamilton)

Jet2.com
Phone 0871 226 1737
Barcelona, Blackpool, Ibiza, Leeds Bradford, Malaga, Milan Bergamo, Murcia, Palma Majorca, Prague, Pisa, Toulouse

Manx2.com
Phone 0870 242 2226
Isle of Man

Wizz Air
www.wizzair.com
Phone 00 48 22 351 9494
Warsaw, Katowice

Zoom
www.zoomairlines.com
Phone 0870 240 0055
Toronto, Vancouver

George Best Belfast City Airport

Recently renamed following the death of Northern Ireland's most famous footballing son, the airport is situated on the main Belfast to Bangor Road, the A2, less than 10 minutes drive from the city centre (see map on inside front cover).

The airport has expanded rapidly in recent years, culminating in the opening of an impressive new terminal building in 2001, following an investment of £22 million. The new site is further away from the rail stop at Sydenham which now lies 10 minutes walk away or a couple of minutes by shuttle bus. **Airport Express 600** bus service into town departs every 20 minutes at peak times from in front of the terminal building. The journey to the Europa Buscentre takes around 15 minutes and currently costs £1.30 single and £2.20 return.

The airport's taxi rank is also in front of the terminal building and the journey into the centre of town is quick and costs around £6. Car hire can be arranged in the arrivals area.

For flight and other airport information telephone (028) 9093 9093 or visit www.belfastcityairport.com. Airlines currently flying from the airport are listed below along with their destinations:

Aer Arann
www.aerarran.com
Phone 0800 587 2324
Cork

British Airways
www.ba.com
Phone 0870 850 9850
Manchester

bmi
www.flybmi.com
Phone 0870 607 0555
London Heathrow

flybe
www.flybe.com
Phone 0871 700 0535
Birmingham, Bristol, Edinburgh, Exeter, Galway, Glasgow, Inverness, Jersey, Leeds Bradford, Liverpool, London Gatwick, Manchester, Newcastle, Robin Hood Doncaster Sheffield, Southampton

British Northwest
www.flybnwa.co.uk
Phone 0871 700 0535
Blackpool, Isle of Man

Euromanx
www.euromanx.com
Phone 0870 787 7879
Isle of Man

Air Berlin
www.airberlin.com
Phone 0870 738 8880
London Stanstead

FERRY SERVICES

Stena Line operate services from Belfast to Stranraer and from Larne to Fleetwood. The Belfast passenger terminal is on Corry Road and bookings can be made by phoning 08705 707070 or via www.stenaline.co.uk. Journey time to Stranraer is 1 hour 45 minutes by HSS fast craft, 3 hours by ferry, and the crossing to Fleetwood takes 8 hours by ferry.

P&O European Ferries operate services between Larne and Cairnryan, and from Larne to Troon. Journey time to Cairnryan is 1 hour by P&O Express and 1 hour 45 minutes by ferry. The crossing time to Troon is 1 hour 45 minutes. Reservations for both services can be made by phoning 0870 2424777 or via www.poirishsea.com.

Norfolkline cross from Belfast to Liverpool. Journey time is 8 hours, and reservations can be made by phoning 0870 600 4321 or visiting www.norfolkline.com..

The Isle of Man Steam Packet Company operates services between Belfast and Douglas (May to September only). Journey time is 2 hours 45 and reservations can be made on 08705 523523 or via www.steam-packet.com.

TRAINS

The public transport system in Northern Ireland is integrated into a single group called Translink which incorporates Northern Ireland Railways (NIR), Ulsterbus and Metro bus services.

NIR operate rail services within Northern Ireland as well as providing the cross-border Enterprise service to Dublin. Central Station on East Bridge Street (p14 K10) stands at the hub of the rail network (see route map opposite). The station is a ten minute walk from the city centre, but passengers carrying a valid rail ticket can travel free into the city centre on any Metro bus, Ulsterbus 500, or Airport Express 600 service that stops outside the main entrance to the station.

Great Victoria Street Station is a more convenient stop than Central for city centre shopping, while Botanic Station is your best bet if you are looking for a night out on the tiles.

Dublin Trains

The train journey to Dublin has been transformed in recent years with investment in new rolling stock and a continuing programme of line improvements which have cut the journey time to around two hours. The first train leaves Central Station at 6.50am, getting into Dublin for 9.05am, and departures are approximately every two hours thereafter, until the last train leaves just after 8pm.

The rest of the network has slowly benefited from an £80m investment programme which has seen the intro-

duction of 23 new trains and the relaying of major sections of track.

Saver Tickets

There is a range of special saver tickets available which allow unlimited rail travel over a set number of days. These tickets, which can be bought at Central Station and other main bus and rail stations, should be purchased before you travel.

A **Freedom of Northern Ireland Travel Pass** is valid for one, three or seven days of unlimited travel on all scheduled bus and rail services within Northern Ireland operated by Northern Ireland Railways, Metro and Ulsterbus, including the Airport Express 300 & 600 services. Cost is currently £14 for one day, £34 for three days and £50 for seven days. The three day ticket is valid for three days travel within a period of eight consecutive days. Tickets are half price for children under 16.

You can take unlimited train journeys within Northern Ireland on Sundays for £5, or £12.50 for a family of two adults and up to four children under the age of 16.

For all rail enquiries phone (028) 9066 6630 or visit the web site at www.translink.co.uk.

BUSES

Metro

Although bus services form part of the integrated transport company, Translink, for practical purposes, you will find yourself boarding either a Metro bus or an Ulsterbus.

Metro was introduced by Translink in February 2005. Designed for ease of use, the simplified Metro network integrated the old Citybus network and greater Belfast Ulsterbus services. The new network is made up of 12 key arterial routes and an additional network of services within the greater Belfast area.

The new fully accessible high frequency service operates throughout the day Monday to Friday (7am-6pm) at 5, 7.5 or 10-minute intervals,

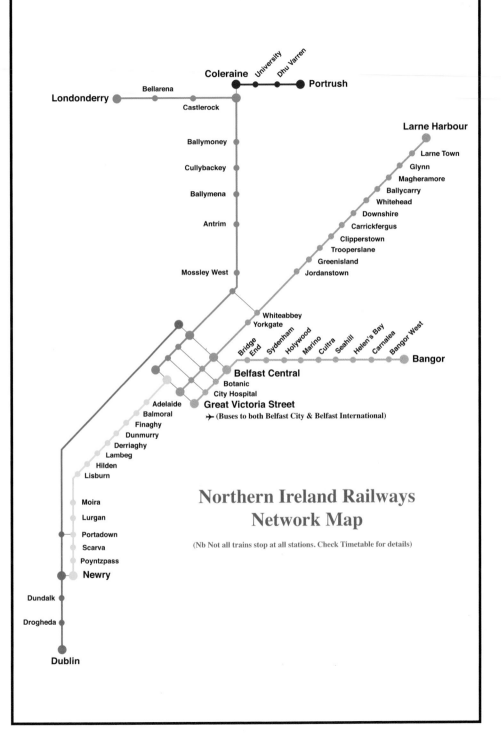

Northern Ireland Railways Network Map

(Nb Not all trains stop at all stations. Check Timetable for details)

Coleraine · University · Dhu Varren · Portrush

Londonderry · Bellarena · Castlerock

Ballymoney
Cullybackey
Ballymena
Antrim
Mossley West

Larne Harbour
Larne Town
Glynn
Magheramore
Ballycarry
Whitehead
Downshire
Carrickfergus
Clipperstown
Trooperslane
Greenisland
Jordanstown

Whiteabbey
Yorkgate

Bridge End · Sydenham · Holywood · Marino · Cultra · Seahill · Helen's Bay · Carnalea · Bangor West · Bangor

Belfast Central
Botanic
City Hospital
Great Victoria Street
✈ (Buses to both Belfast City & Belfast International)

Adelaide
Balmoral
Finaghy
Dunmurry
Derriaghy
Lambeg
Hilden
Lisburn

Moira
Lurgan
Portadown
Scarva
Poyntzpass
Newry

Dundalk
Drogheda

Dublin

Belfast City Centre Bus Departure Points
Timetables: Tel (028) 9066 6630. www.translink.co.uk

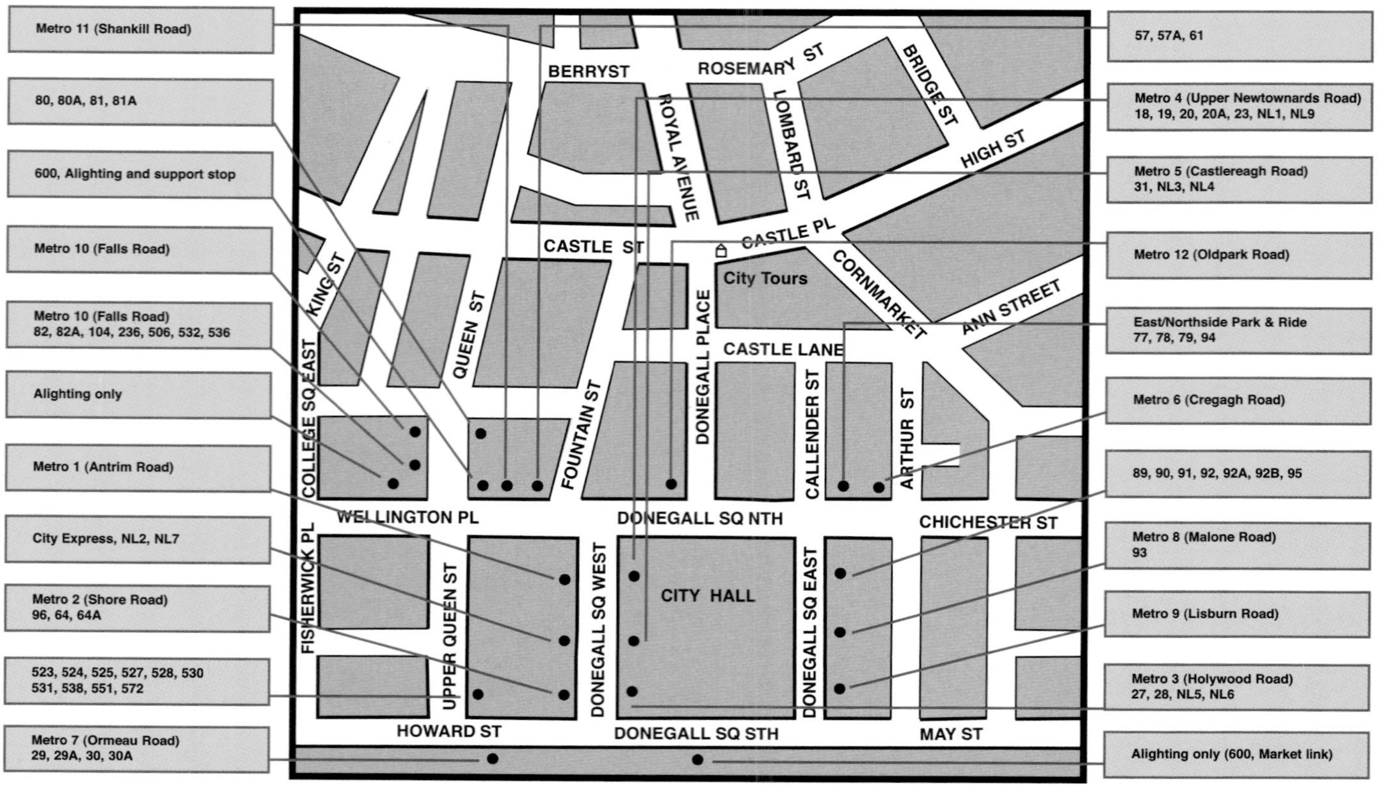

Map labels and bus departure points:

- 57, 57A, 61
- Metro 4 (Upper Newtownards Road) 18, 19, 20, 20A, 23, NL1, NL9
- Metro 5 (Castlereagh Road) 31, NL3, NL4
- Metro 12 (Oldpark Road)
- East/Northside Park & Ride 77, 78, 79, 94
- Metro 6 (Cregagh Road)
- 89, 90, 91, 92, 92A, 92B, 95
- Metro 8 (Malone Road) 93
- Metro 9 (Lisburn Road)
- Metro 3 (Holywood Road) 27, 28, NL5, NL6
- Alighting only (600, Market link)

- Metro 11 (Shankill Road)
- 80, 80A, 81, 81A
- 600, Alighting and support stop
- Metro 10 (Falls Road)
- Metro 10 (Falls Road) 82, 82A, 104, 236, 506, 532, 536
- Alighting only
- Metro 1 (Antrim Road)
- City Express, NL2, NL7
- Metro 2 (Shore Road) 96, 64, 64A
- 523, 524, 525, 527, 528, 530 531, 538, 551, 572
- Metro 7 (Ormeau Road) 29, 29A, 30, 30A

Street names:
BRIDGE ST, HIGH ST, ANN STREET, CHICHESTER ST, MAY ST, ROSEMARY ST, LOMBARD ST, CASTLE PL, CORNMARKET, CASTLE LANE, ARTHUR ST, CALLENDER ST, DONEGALL SQ EAST, ROYAL AVENUE, DONEGALL PLACE, DONEGALL SQ NTH, CITY HALL, DONEGALL SQ STH, BERRY ST, CASTLE ST, FOUNTAIN ST, DONEGALL SQ WEST, QUEEN ST, UPPER QUEEN ST, HOWARD ST, KING ST, WELLINGTON PL, FISHERWICK PL, COLLEGE SQ EAST, City Tours

along the 12 key corridors, and less frequently at other times.

The focal point for Metro services is Belfast City Hall which sits in the middle of Donegall Square. Buses leave from different points, all within the vicinity of the City Hall, and tickets and information for all routes are available from the Metro Kiosk which is situated on Donegall Square West. See page 48 for a map showing all departure points and the corresponding destination. Fares can be paid in cash to the driver when boarding, or a range of multi-journey tickets and travel cards can be purchased beforehand.

A new smart card system called Smartlink allows passengers to purchase journeys in advance and store them on a personal card, offering faster boarding times and considerable discounts. The card can also be used as a weekly or monthly travel card.

Multi-journey cards can be purchased and topped up with journeys in multiples of five. Journeys are valid for three months.

Travel cards provide unlimited travel throughout the Metro network for a period of seven days (currently £14) or one calendar month (currently £53). Cards can be purchased from the Metro Kiosk on Donegall Square West, or from a large number of ticket agents located in newsagents, sweet shops and post offices throughout the city - look for the Metro or Smartlink sign.

For all Metro enquiries phone (028) 9066 6630 or visit Translink web site on www.translink.co.uk.

Ulsterbus

For travel beyond greater Belfast, Ulsterbus operates a comprehensive network of services which connects all the major towns in Northern Ireland, with additional cross-border services to Dublin.

Services operate out of either Laganside Buscentre (p14 K11) or the Europa Buscentre in Glengall Street (p13 J10). Both stations are bright and modern, waiting is done in com-

fort, food and refreshments are available, and staff are on hand to handle any inquiries or booking requirements. North and east bound services depart from Laganside including Portrush and Bangor, while south and west bound buses depart from the Europa Buscentre including Dublin and Derry.

Typical journey times are 1hour 40 minutes for Belfast to Londonderry, and 3 hours for Belfast to Dublin.

For all Ulsterbus enquiries phone (028) 9066 6630 or visit the web site on www.translink.co.uk.

Late Night Services

Metro Nightlink operate eight late services on Saturday nights. Buses depart from Donegall Square West at 1am and 2am and travel to all parts of the city, and on to outlying towns which include Bangor, Comber, Newtownabbey, Antrim, Lisburn, Carrickfergus, Newtownards, Ballynahinch and Downpatrick. Tickets cost £3.50. For further information, phone (028) 9066 6630 or visit the Translink web site at www.translink.co.uk.

Airport Services

Both airports are served by frequent bus services which include the Laganside Buscentre and the Europa Buscentre on their routes. See Air Travel on page 45 for more detail. A bus service to Dublin Airport also leaves from the Europa Buscentre.

Coach Hire

Flexibus and **Ulsterbus** operate fleets of coaches and mini-coaches for private hire, with drivers, for varied travel requirements in and outside Ireland. Wheelchair facilities are provided for the disabled. Information is available from the Europa Buscentre or by telephoning (028) 9023 3933.

City Tours

City Sightseeing run daily open top

bus tours of Belfast, starting from Castle Place at 10am. The tour lasts for approximately 60 minutes and there is a live commentary. There are seven stops in all, and points of interest include political murals, Botanic Gardens and the City Hall. Passengers can get on and off the bus en route, and tickets are valid for 24 hours. Phone (028) 9062 6888.

MiniCoach also run a Belfast City Tour which leaves daily at 10.30am from Belfast International Youth Hostel at 22 Donegall Road. The tour lasts for two hours,and takes in the Falls and Shankill areas, political murals, and many more conventional city landmarks. Cost is currently £9. Phone (028) 9024 6609 for details.

Tours Beyond Belfast

Ulsterbus operate a range of day tours, mainly during the summer months, but a programme is also available for Easter and the May Public Holidays. Destinations are too numerous to mention but include most of the province's resorts and beauty spots. All Ulsterbus Day Tours depart from the Europa Buscentre, Glengall Street. Bookings can be made there in person at the Travelcentre or enquiries can be made on 028 9033 7004.

In addition to their city tour, **MiniCoach**, mentioned above, also do a tour to the Giant's Causeway, departing daily at 9.30am from the International Youth Hostel, returning at approximately 6pm. Cost is £18.

TAXIS

There are taxi ranks at Central Station, the two main bus stations, and in front of the City Hall. Consult the Yellow Pages if you want to book one in advance or try **fonaCAB** on 9033 3333 or **Value Cabs** on 9080 9080.

There has been a recent surge in the popularity of taxis as a means of touring Belfast, and the rest of Northern Ireland for that matter. Taxi tours are a good way of viewing the

City sightseeing tours begin from Castle Place

city's political wall murals, and visiting former trouble spots which may not seem quite as enticing on foot. Prices start from around £20 per hour for up to four people. No extra charge for the running commentary!

All Ireland Tours
Phone (028) 9030 1832
www.allirelandtours.com
Black cab tours of Belfast's political murals and historic buildings, plus separate tours of the north Antrim coast, Derry, and Dublin. City tours at 9.30am, 11.30am, 1.30pm, 3.30pm, 5.30pm & 7.30pm.

Black Taxi Tours
Phone (028) 9064 2264
www.belfasttours.com
Tour Belfast and beyond in a London-style black cab. Daily departures at 10am, 12noon, 2pm, 4pm, 6pm, and 8pm (summer only).

fonaCAB Taxi Tours
Phone (028) 9033 3333
www.fonacab.com
Belfast City tour costs £20 per hour for up to 4 people sharing. Other tours venture farther afield, taking in some of Northern Ireland's principal attractions such as the Giant's Causeway and Carrick-a-Rede Rope Bridge.

Valuecabs Tours by Taxi
Phone (028) 9080 9080

www.valuecabs.co.uk
Belfast City tour costs £20 per hour for up to 4 people sharing. Other tours beyond Belfast include the Giant's Causeway, the Old Bushmills Distillery, and the Ulster American Folk Park. Tours available in normal four seat cars, six seaters which are wheel chair friendly, or executive models such as a Mercedes or BMW for extra comfort.

RIVER TOURS

Lagan Boat Company   `14 K11`
From Donegall Quay
www.laganboatcompany.com
Daily guided boat trips along the River Lagan, including a Titanic Tour. Scheduled departures can be booked by phoning (028) 9024 6609, and private hire can be arranged by phoning (028) 9033 0844. Price £7.

CAR HIRE

Most of the major names in car hire have a presence at both of the city's airports. Details of a centrally located operator are given below:

Budget   `13 J10`
96-102 Great Victoria Street
Phone (028) 9023 0700

CYCLING

Belfast is becoming more bike friendly with several dedicated cycle paths across the city, the main one following the path of the River Lagan. For more information, download **Belfast by Bike** leaflet from www.nationalcyclenetwork.org.uk or phone the sustainable transport movement, Sustrans, on 9043 4569.

Life Cycles   `13 J11`
36-37 Smithfield Market
Winetavern St
Phone (028) 9043 9959
www.lifecycles.co.uk
Cycle hire from £9 per day plus guided cycle tours of Belfast and beyond.

WALKING TOURS

In Belfast, you don't have to leave the city to enjoy a walk in the countryside. A trip to one of the city's many parks (see pages 53-57) offers a tranquil escape. If you fancy something more substantial in terms of exercise, the Lagan Towpath winds its way south for several miles along the river, passing through beautiful meadows and woodland along the way.

If you prefer an organised walking tour, and don't want to venture far from the centre of town, there are several options on offer:

Historic Belfast departs from Belfast Welcome Centre at 47 Donegall Place at 2pm on Wednesday, Friday and Saturday all year round, and on Sundays from June to September. The tour takes you on a 90 minute walk which traces the origins of the city. Cost is £5. Phone (028) 9024 6609 for details.

Belfast Safaris offer a comprehensive range of guided neighbourhood walking tours which take in many lesser known sites, covering aspects such as politics, history, folklore, art and architecture. Also on offer are tailor-made group treks. For more information, phone (028) 9022 2925 or visit www.belfastsafaris.com.

Hotels are a growth industry in Belfast, with several recent openings and more new projects in the pipeline as the city continues to reap the dividends of the ongoing peace process.

Availability is not a major problem but it is a good idea nevertheless to book your accommodation before you travel. If you have acted on impulse, however, and find yourself in Belfast without a room, head for the Belfast Welcome Centre at 47 Donegall Place (telephone 028 9024 6609 or visit www.gotobelfast.com). There you can book accommodation throughout Ireland and the UK.

A cross section of accommodation is listed below. In an effort to keep things simple, the accommodation has been categorised as 'expensive', 'moderate' or 'budget'. Specific prices are not given as they often vary according to the timing of your stay - most of the selected hotels offer special deals, usually relating to weekend stays. Some of the city's guest houses offer rather more interesting accommodation than many of the hotels and a couple of the better ones are included in the moderate category.

Family-run B&B's form the bedrock of budget accommodation, costing around £25 per person sharing, but most are located in the suburbs of the city. Bookings can be made directly or through Belfast Welcome Centre. If you are looking for something cheap but close to the city centre, hostels offer a realistic alternative now that they have shaken off their down-at-heel image. Some have conventional bedrooms but most offer clean and comfortable dorm-style rooms with shared bathrooms. Price normally depends on how many are sharing, but rates are typically around £10 per person per night.

Over the Easter period, and during the summer months from the end of June through to the beginning of September, it is possible to book university accommodation at Queen's. This accommodation is well located and costs around £20 per person per night including breakfast.

All hotels in Northern Ireland are inspected by the Northern Ireland Tourist Board and are given a star rating, from one to five stars, to reflect the standard of the accommodation and the facilities available. Guest houses, which tend to be less expensive than hotels, are graded along similar lines. The appropriate rating is listed below after the name of each establishment. All the hotel and guest house accommodation listed provide rooms with en suite bathroom facilities. A more comprehensive list is available for download at www.gotobelfast.com.

Accommodation Prices

Expensive: Expect to pay in the region of £50 to £80 per night per person sharing, including breakfast. Cheaper rates are usually available at weekends.

Moderate: Expect to pay between £30 and £50 per night per person sharing, including breakfast. Once again, cheaper rates are normally available at weekends.

Budget: Most budget accommodation costs between £15 and £30 per night per person sharing.

Accommodation can be booked directly or via Belfast Welcome Centre. Phone (028) 9024 6609. See page 54 for opening hours.

EXPENSIVE

Europa Hotel**** `13 J10`
Great Victoria Street
Phone (028) 9027 1066
www.hastingshotels.com
Belfast's best known hotel, situated close to the city centre and only a short walk from many popular pubs and restaurants. The 240 bedrooms include the Presidential Suite where Bill and Hillary stayed when they visited Belfast.

Hilton Hotel***** `14 K10`
4 Lanyon Place
Phone (028) 9027 7000
www.hilton.com/belfast
New, high-rise, 195 bedroom hotel situated next door to the Waterfront Hall, overlooking the river. Health club and swimming pool on site.

Malmaison Hotel**** `14 K11`
34-38 Victoria Street.
Phone (028) 9022 0200
www.malmaison.com
Boutique hotel, located in a beautifully converted Victorian warehouse, formerly known as the McCausland Building, which is situated close to the city's main shopping area. 66 bedrooms.

Ten Square**** `13 J10`
10 Donegall Square South
Phone (028) 9024 1001

The Hilton and Waterfront Hall

The stunning Merchant Hotel

www.tensquare.co.uk
Boutique style development occupying an historic building which faces Belfast City Hall. Has attracted many plaudits in the short time it has been open. 22 bedrooms.

Merchant Hotel***   `14 K11`
35-39 Waring Street
Phone (028) 9023 4888
www.themerchanthotel.com
New king of the city's boutique hotels. No expense spared conversion of Grade A listed Ulster Bank HQ. The result is stunning grandeur. Why not complete the rock 'n' roll experience by arranging airport pick-up in the hotel Bentley? 21 bedrooms and 5 suites.

Radisson SAS**   `14 K10`
Cromac Place
Phone (028) 9043 4065
www.radissonsas.com
New development forming an integral part of a major urban regeneration project midway between the city centre and the university area. 120 bedrooms.

MODERATE

An Old Rectory   `20 H7`
148 Malone Road.

Phone (028) 9066 7882
Former rectory, now a guest house situated in one of Belfast's most pleasant suburbs. Four bedrooms.

Ash-Rowan Town House*
12 Windsor Avenue   `20 H8`
Phone (028) 9066 1758
Stylish guesthouse situated in leafy southern suburb, close to Queen's University. Five bedrooms.

Benedicts Belfast*   `13 J9`
7-21 Bradbury Place
Phone (028) 9059 1999
www.benedictshotel.com
Situated in middle of Belfast's 'Golden Mile', close to dozens of bars, restaurants and clubs. 32 bedrooms.

The Crescent Townhouse
13 Lower Crescent   `13 J9`
Phone (028) 9032 3349
www.crescenttownhouse.com
Intimate, 17 bedroomed, hotel situated in an attractive Georgian crescent. Excellent location if you want to be near to some of the best nightlife that Belfast has to offer.

Days Hotel*   `13 J10`
40 Hope Street
Phone (028) 9024 2494
www.dayshotelbelfast.co.uk
244 bedrooms, makes Days the largest hotel in Northern Ireland, but the emphasis is on good quality, city centre, accommodation at affordable prices, with all rooms charged at a flat rate of around £70 per night, which includes free car parking.

Express by Holiday Inn*
106a University Street   `13 J9`
Phone (028) 9031 1909
www.exhi-belfast.com
Reasonably priced accommodation, close to many of the city's main attractions.

Jury's Inn Belfast*   `13 J10`
Great Victoria Street

Phone (028) 9053 3500
www.jurysdoyle.com
Located at one end of the city's Golden Mile, Jury's is a successful Irish chain which is currently exporting its format to several British cities. All rooms are available at a fixed room rate of around £90 per night and can accommodate up to three adults or two adults and two children. 190 bedrooms.

BUDGET

Belfast International Hostel
22 Donegall Road   `12 F9`
Phone (028) 9032 4733
www.hini.org.uk
Modern 38 room hostel with 124 beds. Its location close to the university and many of the city's busiest night spots means that all beds are often booked out. Tour of Belfast city and Giant's Causeway departs daily.

Paddy's Palace   `20 H9`
68 Lisburn Road
Phone (028) 9033 3367
www.paddyspalace.com
Former YWCA. Convenient location for nightlife. Mixture of dorms and private rooms.

Queen's University-Elms Village
78 Malone Road   `20 H7`
Phone (028) 9097 4525
www.qub.ac.uk
University halls offering summer, accommodation in a pleasant location not far from plenty of city night life. Availability from late June to early September. Some en suite facilities.

Stranmillis University College
Stranmillis Road   `20 J7`
Phone (028) 9038 4251
www.stran.ac.uk
University accommodation situated in 46 acres of woodland on the southern side of the city. Available during the summer months. Some en suite facilities available.

Albert Clock
`14 K11`

Queen's Square

Belfast's answer to the Leaning Tower of Pisa was built in 1865 in memory of Queen Victoria's husband, Prince Albert, whose statue forms part of the structure. The 113 feet clock tower was erected on land reclaimed from the river, which explains why it has listed by approximately four feet, giving rise to the local gag that Albert has both the time and the inclination.

Beaches

Belfast may be situated on the shores of Belfast Lough but a day at the beach requires a trip outside the city, the most convenient options being Crawfordsburn and Helen's Bay

The Palm House in Belfast's Botanic Gardens

which are both located between Belfast and Bangor, about twenty minutes away by train or car (see page 47). Northern Ireland's main seaside resorts are Bangor, Newcastle, Portrush and Portstewart.

Belfast Castle & Cave Hill Country Park
`6 H18`

Off Antrim Road

Phone (028) 9077 6925

www.belfastcastle.co.uk

The castle was built by the third Marquis of Donegall in 1870, at a time when Queen Victoria's fondness for Balmoral meant that the Scottish Baronial style was very much in vogue. The marquis's family, the Chichesters, were granted vast tracts of forfeited land during the Plantation of Ulster in 1603. The castle, which was built within a deer park 400 feet up on the slopes of Cave Hill, was donated to the City of Belfast in 1934. A £2m refurbishment was carried out by the city council during the 1980's and facilities now include a heritage centre, antique and craft shop, bar, restaurant, function rooms, and an adventure playground. The grounds of the castle are also open to the public and the relatively gentle climb to the summit of Cave Hill (1,182 feet) is rewarded with a spectacular view over the city and Belfast Lough. There are five caves on the hill and an earthwork called McArt's

Fort where Wolfe Tone and his United Irishmen took their oaths of fidelity prior to the failed 1798 Rebellion.

Belfast Central Library
`13 J11`

Royal Avenue

Phone (028) 9050 9150

Built in 1888 from red sandstone, the library is a mine of valuable research information. Open Monday to Saturday.

Belfast City Hall
`13 J11`

Donegall Square

Phone (028) 9027 0456

Arguably the finest piece of architecture in Belfast, and certainly the city's most recognised landmark, the City Hall is situated in Donegall Square on the site of the former White Linen Hall. Having been granted city status by Queen Victoria in 1888, Belfast decided to respond with a civic building of some magnificence which was intended to reflect the industrial might enjoyed by the city at that time. It was designed by Sir Brumwell Thomas and completed in 1906. The building was constructed in Portland stone in a style somewhat reminiscent of Wren's Saint Paul's Cathedral, with a central copper dome rising 173 feet to dominate the city skyline. A guided tour of the City Hall reveals a sumptuous Italian marble interior which houses many

items of interest, including a mural by Belfast artist, John Luke, symbolising the foundation of the city and its principle industries, and the Charter of Belfast granted by James I on 27th April, 1613. Seats in the council chamber are arranged in a similar style to the House of Commons and additional colour is provided by some of the political debate which takes place within. Paintings in the chamber include a portrait of the Earl of Shaftesbury by the eminent Belfast artist, Sir John Lavery. The grounds of the City Hall are laid out in lawns and flower beds which make it a popular place for shoppers and office workers whenever there is a glimmer of afternoon sunshine. Free guided tours are conducted Mon-Fri 11am, 2pm & 3pm, and Sat 2pm & 3pm.

Belfast Quarters

Locals still talk of Belfast in terms of north, south, east and west but, in an effort to promote tourism, we now have four new Quarters. The **Cathedral Quarter** is a central area in the vicinity of St Anne's Cathedral which has undergone major redevelopment in recent years and is closely associated with the arts, and increasingly with nightlife. South Belfast's **Queen's Quarter** is centred around the university, an affluent area teeming with night life, even during the Troubles. West Belfast's **Gaeltacht**

Odyssey, home of the Belfast Giants, W5 Discovery Centre and and the Sheridan IMAX

Quarter is centred around the Falls Road, a locality synonymous with the Troubles, but now out to promote Irish language and culture. Finally, East Belfast has the **Titanic Quarter**, a 185 acre waterfront regeneration project which aims to transform land previously occupied by Harland & Wolff shipyard, birthplace of the famous ship.

Belfast Exposed - Gallery of Contemporary Photography
23 Donegall Street 　`13 J12`
Phone (028) 9023 0965
Gallery featuring contemporary work of both local and international photographers, with much of the work focusing on social and political themes. *Opening Times: Tues-Sat 11am-5pm*

Belfast Waterfront Hall
See page 58.

Belfast Welcome Centre 　`13 J12`
47 Donegall Place
Phone (028) 9024 6609
www.gotobelfast.com
Impressive new tourist information office, situated close to the City Hall. Facilities include all-Ireland and UK accommodation booking service, tour and event tickets, left luggage, a bureau de change, a well stocked gift shop, and an internet cafe. Plus a vast array of brochures and leaflets in case you are lacking inspiration.

Opening Times: Oct-May, Mon-Sat 9am-5.30pm; June-Sept, Mon-Sat 9am-7pm, Sun 12noon-5pm

Belfast Zoo 　`4 H20`
Off Antrim Road
Phone (028) 9077 6277
www.belfastzoo.co.uk
Belfast Zoo is situated on a fifty acre site on the slopes of Cave Hill, offering panoramic views over the city and Belfast Lough. The zoo is progressive in its outlook, concentrating on the protection of rare and endangered species. Residents include elephants, giraffes, lions, tigers and gorillas but one of the highlights is an underwater viewing position which provides a fish eye view of the sealions and penguins. The zoo is located about four miles north of the city centre and can be reached by Metro bus number 1. *Opening Times: April-Sept 10am-5pm; Oct-March 10am-2.30pm*

Bell Gallery 　`20 H7`
13 Adelaide Park
Phone (028) 9066 2998
www.bellgallery.com
Situated in a Victorian residence in a leafy suburb of south Belfast. Irish painting and sculpture on display. *Open Monday to Friday except for July.*

Botanic Gardens 　`20 J8`
Stranmillis Road

The Botanic Gardens are situated next door to Queen's University, about one mile south of the city centre and, when the sun comes out, there are few better places to escape the hurly burly of city life. The gardens themselves are beautifully laid out but their best known feature is the Palm House which is the earliest surviving example of a curvilinear glasshouse anywhere in the world. It was completed in 1852 by the Dublin ironfounder, Richard Turner, who went on to build the palm house in London's Kew Gardens. The temperate and tropical plants on display include some carnivorous varieties. If the Palm House is not hot enough for you, the gardens also contain the Tropical Ravine where a steamy, artificial climate encourages the growth of orchids, bananas and oranges. The Ravine also houses fish and terrapin ponds. Open daily until dusk.

Crescent Arts Centre
See page 58.

Crown Liquor Saloon
See page 66.

Cultúrlann
See page 58.

Custom House 　`14 K11`
Custom House Square
Designed by Charles Lanyon and completed in 1857, Custom House stands as testimony to the days when Belfast was one of the world's busiest sea ports. The building has undergone a recent refurbishment but the most striking feature remains its sculptured pediment portraying Britannia, Neptune and Mercury looking out over the waterfront. Custom House Square is a new public space used for a series of outdoor summer events.

Divis & Black Mountain
Divis Road
www.belfasthills.org
Out of bounds during the Troubles, this is where we used to watch them watching us. British Army watchtowers and listening posts are no longer

in evidence since control of Belfast's highest hills passed to the National Trust. Panoramic views of the city. Go prepared for all weathers.

Dundonald Ice Bowl
See page 60.

Fernhill House: The People's Museum
Glencairn Road `8 D13`
Phone (028) 9071 5599
Neighbourhood museum which deals with the history of the Shankill area, Home Rule and the two World Wars.
Opening Times: Mon-Sat 10am-4pm; Sun 1pm-4pm. Admission £2

Giant's Ring `26 H11`
Neolithic site featuring the Druid's Dolmen, which stands at the centre of a grass-covered, earth rampart which is 600 feet in diameter and dates back to 2700BC.

Grand Opera House
See page 58.

King's Hall `19 F5`
Lisburn Road
Phone (028) 9066 5225
www.kingshall.co.uk
The King's Hall hosts a wide variety of exhibitions, but the annual highlight is the Balmoral Show which is hosted by the Royal Ulster Agricultural Society in May. This is when the country comes to the city, with all manner of farm animals, rare breeds, special displays, show jumping and outdoor and indoor exhibitions. For further details, visit their website at www.balmoralshow.co.uk.

Lagan Boat Company
See page 50.

Lagan Weir `14 K11`
Donegall Quay
The weir was completed in 1994 and it has made a huge difference to water quality with salmon returning to the river for the first time in many years.

Lagan Valley Regional Park
www.laganvalley.co.uk
Includes a 13 mile stretch of the River Lagan between Stranmillis and Lisburn making it an ideal location for riverside walks or bike rides.

Linen Hall Library `13 J11`
17 Donegall Square North
Phone (028) 9032 1707
www.linenhall.com
Recently refurbished, this is Belfast's oldest library, which was established in 1788 and was originally located in the White Linen Hall before moving to its present location. The library houses many important collections of Irish interest, including its Political Collection, a comprehensive archive on the recent Troubles. The Linen Hall is one of the last survivors of the subscription library movement, but a free day pass is available to any visitor who wishes to browse. The reading room is comfortable and you can enjoy a coffee while immersing yourself in periodicals, magazines and the daily newspapers. The librarians are helpful and the prints which line the wall help to create an atmosphere which evokes a bygone era. *Opening Times: Mon-Fri 9.30am-5.30pm; Sat 9.30am-1pm*

Lyric Theatre
See page 58.

Malone House `26 G3`
Barnett Demesne,
Upper Malone Road
Phone (028) 9068 1246
Beautiful Georgian house which commands spectacular views over Lagan Valley Regional Park. Few better locations to enjoy afternoon tea.

Top 5 For Kids

Odyssey
Belfast Zoo
Ulster Folk Museum
Streamvale Farm
Dundonald Ice Bowl

Sunbathers enjoy a few rays at City Hall

Murals
Belfast is a city of murals, not all political, but most mark out religious and political territory and can often to be found, therefore, in the less salubrious areas of town. Since the outbreak of peace, they have become a major tourist attraction and are usually viewed as part of official sightseeing tours (see page 50), although a trend is developing for walking tours conducted by trained guides who are former republican and loyalist prisoners. **Coiste Political Tours** give the republican perspective - phone (028) 9020 0770 for more details.

Odyssey `14 L12`
Queen's Quay
Phone (028) 9045 1055
www.theodyssey.co.uk
Odyssey is Belfast's £91m landmark project to mark the new millennium, and it is fitting, therefore, to see how it has helped to breathe new life into the city. Odyssey has succeeded on many levels, but none more so than the resident ice hockey team, the Belfast Giant's, who have often played in front of full houses in the 10,000 seater main arena (www.belfastgiants.com). Ice hockey has proved to be a popular family outing, and the support of the new fans was soon rewarded with success on the rink, when the Giants became

A fish out of water at Custom House

UK Superleage champions in only their second season. When the players are off the ice, the arena hosts major concerts, conferences and events.

Other principal attractions include a 14-screen multiplex cinema, an **IMAX** screen which is 60 feet tall and can show films in 3D, twenty lanes of ten pin bowling at **Odyssey Bowl**, and **W5 Interactive Discovery Centre.**

W5 is named after kids' five favourite questions: Who? What? Where? When? Why? (What happened to, 'Are we there yet?'). It is divided into five discovery zones - Wow, Start, Go, See and Do - with 160 interactive exhibits, all designed to stimulate and entertain kids of all ages. Opening hours at W5 are Mon-Sat 10am-6pm, Sun 12pm-6pm. Last admission is at 5pm. Admission is £6 for adults, £4 for kids.

If you need sustenance after all the excitement and activity, the Odyssey Pavilion contains an array of restaurants and bars.

Old Museum Arts Centre
See page 58.

Ormeau Baths Gallery `13 J10`
18a Ormeau Avenue
Phone (028) 9032 1402
www.ormeaubaths.co.uk

Four gallery spaces that have been spawned from a former swimming pool which became surplus to the city's requirements. The main focus is on contemporary art, both local and international. *Opening Times: Tues-Sat 10am-5.30pm. Admission is free.*

Peace Walls `12 F11`
The peace process may be more than ten years old, and normality may be breaking out all over the place. but a large proportion of Belfast's population still lives in areas divided along sectarian lines. For security reasons, the main religious interfaces are separated by high fortifications known as peace walls. Like the political murals mentioned earlier, the walls have become a tourist attraction. There are 17 in all and the best viewing section is on the loyalist Shankill side at Cupar Street where visitors can add their peace messages to those of Bill Clinton and the Dalai Lama.

Public Record Office `19 F6`
68 Balmoral Avenue
Phone (028) 9025 5905
www.proni.gov.uk
The principal repository for records relating to Northern Ireland with documents dating back to the early 17th century. The Public Search Room is a good place to start tracing your family tree although staff do not carry out research on your behalf. The **Ulster**

Historical Foundation on Waring Street may offer further leads. It specialises in history and genealogy research, with particular reference to Ulster, and offers an ancestral research service. Phone (028) 9033 2288.

Queen's University of Belfast
University Road `13 J9`
Phone (028) 9097 5252
www.qub.ac.uk/vcentre
One of Charles Lanyon's finest buildings, the main college was modelled on Magdalen College Oxford and was completed in 1849. The university has recently opened a Visitors' Centre which hosts a programme of exhibitions and sells university memorabilia through its gift shop.

St Anne's Cathedral
Lower Donegall Street `13 J12`
Phone (028) 9032 8332
www.belfastcathedral.org
No point in rushing a good job - this Church of Ireland Cathedral was begun in 1899 but not finished until the 1980's! The architectural style is Hiberno-Romanesque, and the building contains some beautiful stained glass work and stone from every county in Ireland.

St George's Market `14 K10`
May Street
Situated opposite the Waterfront Hall, St George's Market was built by Belfast Corporation in 1890 making it one of Ireland's oldest covered markets. At a cost £4.5m the market was restored in 1997 to its former architectural glory. A variety market takes place every Friday from 6am to 3pm, selling anything from flowers, veg, meat and fish to clothes and antiques. A food and garden market takes place every Saturday from 9am to 3pm..

St Malachy's Church `14 K9`
Alfred Street
Best known for its fine vaulted ceiling which is similar to the one in Henry VII's chapel in Westminster Abbey.

St Peter's Cathedral `13 H11`
St Peter's Square
Phone (028) 9032 7573
www.stpeterscathedralbelfast.com
Constructed in the 1860's, and extensively restored in recent years, this twin spired, Catholic place of worship officially became a cathedral in 1986..

Sinclair Seamen's Church `14 K12`
Corporation Square
Designed by Charles Lanyon in the Venetian style and consecrated in 1853 to serve the spiritual needs of seamen visiting the port of Belfast, this church has become something of a maritime museum. The lectern is shaped like a ship's prow, while the organ sports the port and starboard lights from a Guinness barge from the River Liffey in Dublin. Services begin with the sounding of a bell from HMS Hood which was sunk off Jutland in 1916.

Sir Thomas & Lady Dixon Park
Upper Malone Road `25 D1`
A Mecca for rose growers with 20,000 blooms scenting the air during Rose Week which run takes place every year in July. Other facilities include a Japanese Garden and a children's play area.

Steam Trains Ireland
Phone (028) 9024 6609
www.steamtrainsireland.com
Themed series of steam train journeys on the main rail network, including the Portrush Flyer which runs from Belfast during July and August.

Stormont Parliament Buildings
Upper Newtownards Rd `17 U2`
Situated about three miles from the city centre, Stormont was home to the Northern Ireland Parliament until 1972 when Direct Rule from Westminster was introduced. Both the building and the setting are impressive: the Portland stone construction has a floor space of 5 acres and it stands at the end of a one mile driveway on an elevated position in 300 acres of parkland which is open to the public. The debating chamber was destroyed by fire several years ago but was restored in time to house the new Northern Ireland Assembly, which manages to sit occasionally, whenever the politicians are willing to talk to one another. Stormont Castle is next door, but access to both buildings is restricted for security reasons. Metro numbers 20A and 20 from the city centre.

Streamvale Open Farm `17 U9`
38 Ballyhanwood Road
Phone (028) 9048 3244
Family run farm where you can watch the dairy herd being milked or bottle-feed a lamb. Facilities include a nature trail, pony rides, picnic area, shop and cafe. Open daily from Easter until the end of August, but it is advisable to phone first to check times.

Ulster Hall `13 J10`
Bedford Street
Phone (028) 9032 3900
www.ulsterhall.co.uk
19th century concert and conference hall which houses the magnificent Mulholland Organ. The Ulster Orchestra still give performances in the Hall which is used for a wide range of other concerts and recitals, from classical to rock and pop.

Ulster Folk & Transport Museum
On the A2, Belfast to Bangor Road
Phone (028) 9042 8428
www.uftm.org.uk
Situated just outside Belfast at Cultra, this is a museum of two complementary halves. The Folk Museum gives

Ulster Museum reopens in 2009

Albert Clock - time *and* inclination

a unique insight into Ulster life around the end of the 19th century by reconstructing an ever-increasing number of houses, workshops, mills, shops, schools, churches and other public buildings which have been removed from all parts of the province and rebuilt stone by stone within the rural setting of the museum, which overlooks Belfast Lough. Inside most of the buildings you will find a blazing peat fire and a friendly and informative attendant. The centre piece of the Transport Museum is the Irish Railway Collection which is housed within a huge new gallery. Other galleries display a diverse range of exhibits which include early Ulster-built planes and motorbikes, a De Lorean motor car assembled in Belfast in 1982, and an exhibition dedicated to the Titanic, which was built in Belfast in 1912 and sank on her maiden voyage to New York with the loss of 1,500 lives. *Open Mon-Fri 10am-5pm; Sat 10am-6pm; Sun 11am-6pm. Combined admission is £7 per adult, £4 children*

Ulster Museum `20 J8`
Botanic Gardens
Phone (028) 9038 3000
Situated about a mile south of the city centre, Northern Ireland's national museum is currently undergoing a major refurbishment programme and is due to reopen in 2009.

Belfast, like the rest of Ireland, is proud of its artistic tradition and the arts have been going from strength to strength in recent years thanks to considerable investment in new venues, and continuing financial support from public and private sectors.

The opening of Belfast's Waterfront Hall in 1997 added a new jewel to the city's entertainment crown but the cultural highlight of the year undoubtedly remains the **Belfast Festival at Queen's** which normally runs from the last week in October through to the first week in November. For more than forty years, it has been a world class festival of culture which attracts many international artists from the world of theatre, dance, music and comedy who perform at venues in and around Queen's University. The festival is currently suffering a funding crisis however, and the staging of the 2007 event is under threat unless more public funds are forthcoming. The full festival programme is usually available from September. For more information phone (028) 9097 1197 or visit the web site at www.belfastfestival.com.

Since 2000, the city's up and coming Cathedral Quarter has hosted its own alternative arts festival in May, and it attracts some high profile names from the world of music and literature. For more information, phone (028) 9023 2403 or visit www.cqaf.com.

West Belfast has been hosting a community festival of its own every since August 1988. **Feile an Phobail** includes a varied programme of drama, comedy, music, sport and political debate, culminating in a colourful parade up the Falls Road. Phone (028) 9031 3440 or visit their website at www.feilebelfast.com

If you are planning a night out at the theatre, cinema or a performance of live music or comedy, the Belfast Telegraph is a good source of up to date info.

THEATRE

Black Box `13 K11`
18-22 Hill Street

Phone (028)9024 4400
www.blackboxbelfast.com
New 275 seat performance space located in the Cathedral Quarter. Venue for drama, comedy and music.

Belfast Waterfront Hall `14 K11`
2 Lanyon Place
Box Office (028) 9033 4455
www.waterfront.co.uk
When Belfast Waterfront Hall opened its doors in January 1997, it marked the completion of the most significant civic building to be built in Belfast since the City Hall was completed in 1906. In common with many other major public buildings, the development attracted its fair share of controversy, with the final cost exceeding £30m. In terms of Belfast's renewed self-confidence, however, the investment has paid valuable dividends. The Main Auditorium seats 2,235 and hosts an eclectic mix of artistic performance, from major symphony concerts to rock, pop and comedy. The Studio space and additional meeting rooms provide state of the art facilities which help to make Belfast a popular choice for hosting conferences.

Crescent Arts Centre `13 J9`
2-4 University Road
Phone (028) 9024 2338
www.crescentarts.org
Converted Victorian school which hosts workshops in all kinds of dance, circus, music and other artistic skills as well as staging regular studio performances and exhibitions.

Cultúrlann `12 F10`
216 Falls Road
Phone (028) 9096 4180
www.culturlann.ie
Irish language arts and cultural centre

The refurbished Grand Opera House

which stages most of its theatrical productions in Irish, although simultaneous translations are usually available to those people with little or no understanding of the language.

Grand Opera House `13 J10`
Great Victoria Street
Phone (028) 9024 1919
www.goh.co.uk
Recently reopened after a £9 million refurbishment and extension, the Grand Opera House remains a monument to the extravagance of Victorian theatre designer, Frank Matcham. The turrets and curlicues which make up the facade reflect an Eastern influence which is also evident inside where sculpted elephants support the boxes and the lavishly painted ceiling. Although the first opening curtain was in 1895, the Victorian splendour owes much to painstaking restoration carried out to repair serious bomb damage during the Troubles. The Opera House stages a wide variety of theatre, opera, music, dance, and comedy. There are special facilities for wheelchair users and an induction loop system relays non-musical performances to hearing aid users.

Lyric Theatre `20 J7`
55 Ridgeway Street
Box Office (028) 9038 1081
www.lyrictheatre.co.uk
Founded by Mary O'Malley in the 1950's, the Lyric is Northern Ireland's only repertory theatre, presenting a broad range of classical and contemporary plays with a particular emphasis on Irish works. The theatre aims to fulfil a broad role, offering fifty weeks a year of varied programming ranging from live music, dance and comedy events to co-productions with local theatre companies and the best of Irish theatre. Situated on the banks of the Lagan in the heart of Stranmillis village, about two miles from the city centre. Access is available for patrons with special needs and the auditorium is equipped with a loop induction system.

Old Museum Arts Centre `13 J11`
7 College Square North
Box Office (028) 9023 3332

www.oldmuseumartscentre.org
Intimate theatre space and gallery with an avant-garde artistic policy. Productions include drama, dance and poetry and there are regular workshops and exhibitions of art and photography.

COMEDY

Belfast is usually included on the touring schedule of the major comedy acts who tend to play the main theatrical venues such as the Waterfront Hall and the Grand Opera House. Come November, the Belfast Festival at Queen's attracts a plethora of comedy acts to town including many of the critical successes seen a few weeks earlier at the Edinburgh Fringe.

Several Belfast pubs have staged live comedy but Tuesday night at the **Empire** on Botanic Avenue is the mainstay, made famous by local boy made good, Paddy Kielty who acted as compere for many years. The evening usually showcases a combination of local talent and some bigger fish drawn from comedy circuits in London and Dublin. A good laugh is usually guaranteed.

CINEMA

The Northern Ireland Film Commission was set up in 1997 to promote Northern Ireland as a potential location for film makers. Several movies have been made locally in recent years including Divorcing Jack and Titanic Town.

For many years the number of Belfast cinemas seemed to be in inexorable decline, but the advent of the multiplex has reversed this trend and there are now dozens of screens to choose from around the city, including the recent arrival of an **IMAX** screen at the Odyssey complex. Most, however, concentrate on the mainstream Hollywood releases and, as a consequence, many cinemas end up showing the same film. The **Queen's Film Theatre** on University Square is the main exception to this rule, catering to followers of European cinema as well as screening many cult classics. For more information, phone 9097 1097

Audiences flock to the Waterfront Hall

or visit www.queensfilmtheatre.com.

The Belfast Film Festival is in its infancy but is organised around the end of March in conjunction with the QFT and several multi screens around town. For more details, visit the fwebsite at www.befastfilmfestival.org.

MUSIC

Belfast is steeped in musical tradition, with the likes of Van Morrison and James Galway among its famous sons. The city is regularly included on the itinerary of these and countless other celebrated international artists and entertainers.

For lovers of classical music, the **Ulster Orchestra** performs a series of concerts throughout the year at the Ulster Hall and at the Waterfront Hall. The orchestra continues to grow in reputation, both at home and abroad, and has performed several times at the Henry Wood Promenade Concerts in London's Royal Albert Hall. For details of concerts and recordings, contact the ticket office on (028) 9066 8798.

Queen's School of Music hosts regular daytime and evening recitals

in the Harty Room. Phone (028) 9097 5337 for details.

For opera buffs, the annual highlight is the **Castleward Opera Season** which is Northern Ireland's answer to Glyndebourne. Performances throughout June. For more details phone (028) 9263 9545 or visit www.castlewardopera.com.

It will come as no surprise to learn that Belfast pubs provide the main platform for local bands and musicians. There are dozens of such venues and many of them are listed in the Pubs section on pages 64-72. A good choice of rock, jazz, folk and blues is usually on offer. Most of the major rock and pop concerts in Belfast take place at the Odyssey Arena or the Waterfront Hall, but Botanic Gardens has also been used for several large outdoor concerts in recent years, the largest of which was a widely acclaimed performance by U2. For lovers of jazz, the annual highlight is the **Holywood International Jazz Festival** which usually takes place in June and manages to attract some famous names. Phone (028) 9076 8563 or visit their website at www.holywoodjazzfestival.com.

Northern Ireland punches well above its weight when it comes to sport, providing many household names such as George Best, Alex Higgins, Barry McGuigan and Mary Peters. Facilities tend to be good considering the size of population, and the opportunity exists to participate in most sporting activities. The Sports Council is a useful source of information - phone (028) 9038 1222 or visit www.sportni.net.

ATHLETICS

International athletics meetings are held at the Mary Peters Track which is in the Malone Playing Fields, just off the Upper Malone Road. The track is in the care of the City Council and is available for public use (www.niathletics.org). The most popular event in the athletics calendar is Belfast City Marathon which is staged in May, and attracts more than 10,000 runners. For an application form, phone (028) 2587 2828 or visit their website at www.belfastcitymarathon.com. Another major annual event is the International Cross Country which attracts a world class field to the Stormont Estate in January.

ICE HOCKEY

Northern Ireland has been crying out for years for live sport which can entertain all the family, in state of the art facilities, free from any sectarian overtones. Ice hockey arrived in town in 2000 and the fans have taken to it big time, packing into the Odyssey Arena to watch the Coors Belfast Giants. The team were Elite League champions in 2006. The season runs from September to April and tickets currently cost £14 for adults and £8 for children. The box office number is (028) 9073 9074 and their web address is www.belfastgiants.com.

Belfast Giants play the Odyssey

ICE SKATING

Dundonald Ice Bowl
111 Old Dundonald Road   **17 V9**
Phone (028) 9080 9100
www.theicebowl.com
The Ice Bowl boasts Ireland's only Olympic sized rink which is used for ice hockey as well as skating. Lessons are available from highly trained resident instructors. Other facilities on site include 30 lanes of ten pin bowling, Indiana Land, a jungle themed play area for children, and Pirates Adventure Golf.

FOOTBALL

The English Premiership attracts much more interest locally than the domestic football programme, but five Belfast teams currently play in the Irish League: Linfield play at Windsor Park, Glentoran at the Oval, Cliftonville at Solitude, Crusaders at Seaview, and newly promoted Donegal Celtic at Suffolk. Most league matches are played on Saturdays.

On the international front, Northern Ireland have been going through a lean spell since qualifying for two World Cups during the 1980's. They recently acquired an unwelcome world record for their failure to score a goal. This drought was finally broken under their new manager, Lawrie Sanchez, and the team have recently enjoyed some

success with home victories over England and Spain. International matches are played at Windsor Park.

The Irish Football Association can be contacted on (028) 9066 9458 or www.irishfa.com

GAELIC GAMES

The main venue for watching gaelic football, hurling and camogie is Casement Park on the Andersonstown Road. The nine counties of Ulster compete in the Ulster Championships with the winner going on to compete for a place in the all Ireland finals which are played at Croke Park in Dublin in September each year. Tyrone were football champions in 2005. Most matches are played on Sunday afternoons, and the Ulster Council of the Gaelic Athletic Association can be contacted on (028) 9038 3815 or www.gaa.ie

GOLF

Unlike many other countries, golf is not seen as an elitist game in Ireland. Northern Ireland is lucky enough to have two of the finest links courses in the world at Royal Portrush, which has staged the British Open, and Royal County Down which enjoys a breathtaking setting where the mountains of Mourne sweep down to the sea. Nicklaus, Palmer and Player have all been in attendance recently to compete in the British Seniors Open.

Malone Golf Club in Belfast is one of the best parkland courses in Ireland and Belvoir Park gives Malone a good run for its money. There are courses to suit players of all abilities and green fees tend not to be prohibitively expensive, especially at the municipal courses. A full list is available in the Yellow Pages, but a few of the better courses in and around Belfast are listed below. All are private clubs but visitors are welcome, especially during the week, although it is advisable to phone beforehand.

If you want to see how the game really should be played, take a trip to the Irish Open which is one of the leading tournaments on the European Tour, attracting many of the world's top players. The event is normally staged in May and will take place at Adare Manor in Limerick until 2009.

Belvoir Park Golf Club `27 L5`
73 Church Road, Newtownbreda
Phone (028) 9064 6714
6,476 yards. Par 71

Knock Golf Club `17 V11`
Upper Newtownards Road
Phone (028) 9048 3825
6,407 yards. Par 70

Malone Golf Club `25 E2`
240 Upper Malone Road.
Phone (028) 9061 2758
6,656 yards. Par 71

Shandon Park Golf Club `16 R9`
73 Shandon Park.
Phone (028) 9080 5030
6,011 yards. Par 70

Newforge Lane Golf Centre
22 Newforge Lane `26 H4`
Phone (028) 9068 3174.
Driving range with 26 floodlit bays open until 10pm every day.

GYMNASIUMS

It is a partly a legacy of the divisions brought about by the Troubles, but Belfast is endowed with more public leisure centres than you are likely to find anywhere else of a similar size in the world. There are more than a dozen dotted around the city (see Yellow Pages for a full list), and most enjoy the benefits of hi-tech fitness equipment, and many have their own swimming pool, sauna & solarium,

squash courts, and football pitches.

HORSE RACING

Ireland is famous throughout the world for producing thoroughbred race horses and Northern Ireland has two courses where you can go along and enjoy a flutter. The annual highlights in the racing calendar are the Ulster Grand National which is run at Downpatrick in March, and the Ulster Derby, which is a more fashionable affair, run at Down Royal, near Lisburn (downroyal.com), in June. Both courses stage frequent meetings throughout the year.

RUGBY

Lansdowne Road in Dublin is the headquarters of the Irish Rugby Football Union and the home venue for all of Ireland's international matches. The highlight of the year is the Six Nations Championship which takes place from January to March when Ireland take on England, Scotland, Wales, France and Italy. Thousands of away fans invade Dublin for what is a great social occasion and, regardless of Irish form, tickets are very difficult to acquire.

Ravenhill Stadium is the HQ of the Ulster branch of the union, and 1999 will long be remembered for Ulster's victory in the European Cup. The team won the Celtic League title in 2006. For ticket info, phone (028) 9049 3222 or go to www.ulsterrugby.com

SWIMMING

As mentioned earlier, the city is very well off when it comes to swimming pools. A couple of the main ones are listed below:

Grove Leisure Centre `14 K14`
York Road

The first hole at Royal County Down

Phone (028) 9035 1599
Gala Pool - 25 x 12.8m - with capacity for 800 spectators.

Olympia Leisure Centre `19 F7`
Boucher Road
Telephone (028) 9023 3369
25m Swimming Pool

TEN-PIN BOWLING

Dundonald Ice Bowl `17 V9`
111 Old Dundonald Road.
Phone (028) 9080 9100
30 lanes

Odyssey Bowl `14 K11`
Queens Quay
Phone (028) 9046 7030
20 lanes

TENNIS

Since most clubs are privately run for the benefit of their members, the most realistic option is a game at one of the city's leisure centres. The best public facility is the Belfast Indoor Tennis Arena which has 4 indoor courts and is situated in Ormeau Park, off the Ormeau Embankment. Telephone (028) 9045 8024.

You may need to kick off your Manolos to pound the pavements of Belfast in the rain, but even the fussiest of fashionistas will find something to buy in the rejuvenated city centre. Day time business austerity quickly transforms into nighttime glamour. That Northern Irish, baggy suited, fashion reject, otherwise known as Belfast man, is also sharpening up and, with the right light and a couple of sauvignon blancs, is looking good.

Royal Avenue

CastleCourt, on Royal Avenue, with its integrated car parking merits a mention as it heralded Belfast's resurgence. **Debenham's** department store's expansion into diffusion designer clothing has ensured their survival - in no small way due to the Irish based designer, John Rocha. Most of the other shops are branches of High Street chains and the centre badly needs a boost but is still teeming with mall rat teenagers and families. Although many of the boutiques aim for the younger market, **Laura Ashley, Gerry Weber** and **Olsen** can still attract a more mature shopper. **TK Maxx** can occasionally unearth a designer bargain, but only to the dedicated rummager. On the corner, **Virgin** stocks the usual mega deals for multimedia relaxation. Irish competition, in the form of **Golden Discs** on Donegall Place, concentrates on music CDs. Cross Royal Avenue onto Rosemary Street to find **Fresh Garbage** which must be Belfast's longest survivor, confirming that old hippies never die. Just off Rosemary Street is **Liberty Blue** which sells individual, casual urban wear and is staffed by the unsurliest teenagers you could ever hope to meet. Nip through Donegall Arcade, to the adjacent High Street, as it does contain shopping delights, despite outward appearances, in the shape of **Brazil** for women and **Rio** for men. Younger, cheaper fashion needs are catered for in **Paranoid** and **Envy** on the High Street, and the

clubby **NV** in Castle Place. High Street is now dominated by the spacious, airy and well laid out **Dunnes Stores**. Their linen suits are a must buy and the home section is looking very Sunday supplement urban living desirable. The cafe ain't bad either.

Cornmarket

Another branch of **NV** is on Ann Street, with a huge **New Look** for those with more dash than cash. Literary types can root through **Easons**. In Arthur Street back towards the Cornmarket the lycra clad young can head to French chain, **Morgan**, or **Pulse** which stocks the likes of Diesel, Miss Sixty and G Star. Funky footwear is found in the adjoining **DV8**. At the bottom is the large, glass fronted and rather isolated looking **Benetton**. Hedonistic spending can continue in **USC** with it's designer labels, or reliable chain, **River Island**, before coming back to the main thoroughfare. This area is set to receive a massive boost with the opening of the £320m **Victoria Square** retail development. **House of Fraser** and **H&M** are among the new faes in town.

City Hall

Coruna's claim to fame has been the success of their football team in La Liga and in the European arena. However, it is also the home to **Zara,** the most successful womenswear company in the world. Belfast has its own Donegall Place branch of classic contemporary styling at reasonable prices for women, men, *y los ninos*. The

CastleCourt Shopping Centre

English reply to this Spanish invader is the sassy **Karen Millen** shop opposite the City Hall. The clothes often grace the pages of glossy magazines and the backs of the N.Ireland glitterati.Squeezed between this and Kate Moss favourite **Topshop** is the Barcelona based **Mango**, which like its neighbour produces cat walk copy fashion of high quality at a low price. Pregnant woman can keep themselves looking good at **Formes** on Fountain Street. A major transformation has been the area between Wellington Place and Howard Street, where the Hoxton fin is ubiquitous. Wedding list favourite, for the past decade, **Equinox**, is in Howard Street. While you are sorting out the list you could do worse than cajole him into **Thomas Jewellers** for the ring. Between the two lies the **Bureau.** English favourites are covered by the resurgently trendy Burberry, and the reliable classic quirkiness of Paul Smith. Uberhip Japanese label Evisu features strongly. If it is shoes you want, next door's **Hole** will kit your feet out in style. The Bureau's rather pompously titled offshoot, **Grand Magasin** in Wellington Street, is a large, relaxed oasis of urban fashion with surprisingly friendly but seriously stylish staff. Serious drooling and credit card damage likely. At the corner of nearby Upper Queen Street, **Spires** houses a new religious fervour - shopping - rather than its past glory as a Presbyterian centre. Longstanding favourite **Carter,** for those who value expensive designer discretion, neighbours the **Clothes Agency,** a place that matches vintage clothing with modern accessories. **Coppermoon** is crammed with a mishmash of presents, jewellery, pictures and handbags. The adjacent, well stocked **Ltd** offers ghetto fabulous gear. Adjoining is renovated **Timberland** for the outdoor look in town. Back on Wellington Place, brash newcomer **Clockwork Orange** will ensure the droogs look their clubby best, while nearby **Animal** aims for the surfer look.

Sunkissed skin and sunbleached blonde locks are your own responsibility. Alternatively you may prefer the preppy look with Hilfiger Denim.

Don't think you get to spend your hard earned money on yourself. Designer-clad children are this year's fashion accessories. **Xero** will sort out your DKNY and D&G junior. Similarly, in Arthur Street, your child can step out in co-ordinated style in the likes of **Diesel**, and on the Lisburn Road **Harper 2** and **Zeo American** will make sure the little darlings empty your wallet. The continuation of Wellington Place brings you to Chichester Street and the sumptuous, aptly named **Boudoir**, stuffed with sexy Chloe and Avoca. Bell entry can be off putting for **Michelle O'Doherty's** store. But although expensive, with heavy emphasis on small collections of the most exclusive designers such as Vivienne Westwood, the staff are really friendly (remember this is Belfast not trustafarian Mayfair) and the clothes exquisite, with fabulous end of season reductions.

Bedford Street

Now heading south past the City Hall towards the Golden Mile, your now weary feet will bring you to Bedford Street. Shirtmakers **Smyth & Gibson** represent quality in Irish linen. Complete the retail therapy by visiting **Steenson's** for individual designed jewellery. Belfast has an extensive choice in jewellery, the most venerable of which is **Malcolm's** on May Street and the Lisburn Road, and the glitzier **Lunns** in the Queen's Arcade and now **Lunns2** on Royal Avenue. Restaurants and bars line the Golden Mile of Great Victoria Street, but little opportunity for sober spending.

Lisburn Road

Demographics influence consumer spending. It is interesting that Belfast's southern suburb is choc full of clothes for the over 25's earning over £25K. The collections are not brash, one season designer wear, nor trashy clubby, but classic with a twist. Far more so than other cities, and may also reflect the restaurant and late bar scene rather than night club influence. There is a distinct danger that those with money will not bother going into town. The shopping is almost entirely female oriented. At **BT9** and **Brazil** in Shaftesbury Square women can choose classic workwear and weekend wear but the strength of the shop is their funky, unusual evening orientated wear. If there ever is a serious department store like Brown Thomas or Selfridges, the Lisburn Road corridor of boutiques may not survive. The burgeoning success of these designer outlets is testimony to the financial clout professional Belfast women can wield. **Ivanna, Mary and Martha, Statement at Margaret Giboney,** and **Courtyard** keep the Continental flair alive. In **Koko,** smart formal clothes are interspersed with the achingly trendy and exclusive ranges. **Panache** lures the professional woman in for work and weekend. Around the corner from Tatu is the modern, spacious sophisticated **Emporio,** and Maxmara-related **Marina Rinaldi** for the more voluptuous. Opposite, a row of shops includes **Helen Mac Alinden** for simple well cut linens, **Harper** which stocks the politicians favourite, Louise Kennedy, and **Bang & Olufson** to keep the gadgets fiends amused. Fashionable feet are not forgotten at trendy **Rojo** and luscious **Honey** which also stocks cute accessories. Middle class branches of **Maxmara, Benetton, Space NK,** and **Hobbs** have chosen the Lisburn Road to germinate along with **Eden Park** for the rugby wearing middle England type. Men get a quick look in at the **Living Room** and **Clarke & Dawe. Blush** is the ultimate place for evening and wedding wear with **Posh Frocks** catering more for cocktail dress occasion wear. Nearby **Object Lounge** provides designer furniture and Alessi driven

Belfast male turns his back on retail therapy

Christmas wish lists.

Throughout the year south Belfast stores burr with the sound of gold cards being swiped. The rest of the city may have less ching ching but is still buzzing. Retail rejuvenation has even reached **St. George's Market** which has become a genuinely exciting food market. City centre stalwart **Sawyers** in the Fountain Centre is Belfast's longest standing delicatessen and it's still holding its own against stiff competition back up on the Lisburn Road, where **M&S Food** and scrumptious delis such as **Arcadia** and **Swantons** are challenging the Ulster fry.

Donegall Pass has always had a number of antique shops but is now being promoted as Belfast's antiques sector. There are several greenbelt shopping centres, mostly centred around one of the supermarket chains. **Forestside** in Upper Galwally, and **Sprucefield** off the M1 near Lisburn, also supplement the Donegall Place branch of Northern Ireland favourite, **Marks & Spencers**. Both Ormeau Road with **Evelin Brandt** and **La Femme,** and Bloomfield Road with the **White Bicycle** and **Peel Fashions** provide individual fashion pampering in intimate boutique surroundings.

A design-savvy metropolis? You'd better believe it.

It seems that wherever you go in the world these days, an Irish pub is rarely far away. Ireland rightly has a reputation for great pubs and Belfast certainly upholds that tradition. The pub represents the heart and soul of the city's social life and there are hundreds to choose from. Belfast may have had more than its fair share of trouble over the years but its citizens have never lost their appetite for 'a good night's craic' which goes a long way to explaining the popularity and the appeal of the city's pubs.

There are several historic pubs dotted around the city centre, and an increasing number of modern ones which reflects the growing trend for cafe bars. Anybody familiar with the development of the pub and bar scene in Dublin over the past ten years will recognise that Belfast has lagged behind its southern neighbour, but the gap is narrowing, and the opening of bars such as **Tatu** and **Apartment** has helped to breathe some cosmopolitan air into the city.

The list below tries to point you in the direction of some of the best watering holes but, if you feel strongly that any have been wrongly included or unfairly omitted, feel free to let us know (see page 2 for contact details).

Most of the pubs listed serve food and many stage live music. To find out who is playing when and where, pick up a copy of the Big List, a free guide to what's on which is published every four weeks and is available in many shops, cafes and venues around town. Alternatively, check the Belfast Telegraph.

The list below is NOT broken into categories as so many of Belfast's bars and clubs fall into more than one bracket. Many bars have their own nightclub where you can drink and dance until 1am, and much later in some cases. Opening hours have also been omitted due to the relaxed nature of the licensing

laws in Belfast. Extensions are frequently applied to normal opening times which are 11.30am to 11pm Monday to Saturday, and 12noon to 10pm on Sundays. Half an hour drinking up time is allowed after these hours.

Beer consumption is dominated by two major brewers, Guinness and Bass, although a local real ale alternative is provided by Hilden which is brewed in Lisburn. If spirits are your favourite tipple, it is well worth noting that Northern Irish measures are 40% bigger than those served in English pubs!

There are good pubs all over Belfast but it is fair to say that the bulk of the really popular ones are located in the south of the city, especially around the university area. This phenomenon gave rise to the concept of Belfast's 'golden mile', an area which runs south from Great Victoria Street to the bottom of the Malone Road. This stretch still contains many of the city's best bars and restaurants but the centre of gravity is continually shifting as areas such as the Lisburn Road, the city centre, and the Cathedral Quarter stake their claim to a slice of the action.

Finally, if you like to keep on

Cafe Vaudeville on Arthur Street

the move but you aren't sure where you are going, you might like to try an organised pub crawl. **Bailey's Historical Pub Tour of Belfast** does what the title implies, starting upstairs at the Crown Bar. The entrance is on Amelia Street. Tours run from May to October, every Thursday at 7pm, and every Saturday at 4pm. The tour lasts for about 2 hours and covers six pubs. Cost is £6 per head, excluding booze! Group tours can be booked all year round. Times are subject to change, so it is advisable to phone (028) 9268 3665 beforehand to check availability. For more information, visit www.belfastpub-tours.com.

If you would rather organise your own pub crawl, then feel free to work your way through the list below!

am:pm
67-69 Botanic Avenue   `13 J9`
Phone (028) 9023 9443
38-42 Upper Arthur Street   `13 J11`
Phone (028) 9024 9009
Two contemporary cafe bars, both relative newcomers, with a strong emphasis on imaginative food and chilled out interiors. Good choice for Sunday brunch.

Apartment   `13 J11`
2 Donegall Square West
Phone (028) 9050 9777
www.apartmentbelfast.com
Ask locals where the centre of the city is, and most will say Donegall Square, an area dominated by Belfast's magnificent City Hall. By day, the streets are crammed with office workers and shoppers but, by night, an eerie silence traditionally descended. That stark contrast has been eroded, however, thanks in large part to the opening of Apartment which instantly became one of the busiest bars in town. Apartment is a large development, but it is easy to walk past the small cafe bar on the ground floor, oblivi-

ous to the fact that the upper floor extends into several adjoining premises, providing acres of eating and drinking space and some attractive views of the City Hall. The layout is divided into several distinct spaces, but the use of dark wood and brown leather are recurring themes which help to give an air of warmth and comfort. Busy by day with coffee drinkers and lunchtime diners, and long into the night, Apartment looks set to remain in the vanguard of Belfast's new breed of style conscious bars.

Auntie Annie's Porterhouse
44 Dublin Road   `13 J10`
Phone (028) 9050 1660
Auntie Annie's proves the old adage that when it comes to property the three most important aspects are location, location and location. This is a slightly strange mix of Irish theme bar and live music venue, but it's in the right place to attract a passing crowd from nearby cinemas and restaurants.

Bar Bacca   `13 J10`
43 Franklin Street
Phone (028) 9023 0200
www.barbacca.com
Belfast meets Bangkok, with a bar somewhat reminiscent of the famous Buddha Bar in Paris. The Thai imagery runs throughout and, aided by low lighting, soothing music, comfortable seating and a cocktail or two, it is almost possible to enjoy a spiritual experience - that is until the place becomes packed out later in the evening and there's little room left for you and your karma to get to the bar.

Bar Twelve   `13 J9`
13 Lower Crescent
Phone (028) 9032 3349
A bar which would sit comfortably in this very attractive Georgian crescent if it weren't for the fact that it was recently painted purple. Redeemed by a calm and comfortable interior which makes it a good

Students of 'urban living' compare notes at Apartment

stopping off point if you are making your way from the city centre to the university area.

Basement Bar & Grill   `13 J11`
18 Donegall Square East
Phone (028) 9033 1925
Handy hideaway situated across the road from the City Hall. Busy lunchtime trade and live music to pull the customers in after dark.

Benedict's   `13 J9`
7-21 Bradbury Place
Phone (028) 9059 1999
Hotel and bar development where much of the gothic style interior seems to have come from an architectural salvage yard judging by the abundance of carved wood and stained glass. This is a large bar to fill but its location and a weekly programme of musical events usually guarantees a brisk trade.

Botanic Inn   `20 H7`
23 Malone Road
Phone (028) 9050 9740
The Bot remains a Belfast institution despite being demolished and totally rebuilt a few years ago. Its location close to Queen's University guarantees a busy bar throughout

the day and night. The blend of traditional and modern styles attracts a wide cross section of customers, young and not so young, students and professionals. A good place to watch live football on a big screen. Live music downstairs and disco upstairs help to pack the punters in.

Bridge Bar   `13 J10`
35-43 Bedford Street
Phone (028) 9072 7890
Refurbished and renamed, but still part of the Wetherspoon's chain. Not many pubs display their prices in the front window, but here you even get to compare prices with nearby watering holes. Cheap drink, a good choice of real ales, and a solid reputation for food which is served from breakfast at 10am until half an hour before closing. A suc-

---

Top 5 Bars For Food

The John Hewitt
Apartment
The Errigle
am:pm
The King's Head

The Cloth Ear has added to the buzz around the Cathedral Quarter

cessful combination, judging by the fact that it's busy throughout the day.

Cafe Vaudeville `13 J11`
25-39 Arthur Street
Phone (028) 9043 9160
If you are familiar with Dublin bars, think Cafe en Seine. If not, then expect the sober facade of a former bank and an opulent, *art nouveau* interior on a theatrical scale (some locals cruelly refer to it as 'Cafe Gaudyville'). Bar, bistro and cafe,

Tales of the riverbank at Cutters

all in one - even has its own Bolli Bar on first floor. Popular meeting place for coffee and lunch. Live jazz, blues, salsa, and resident DJ's come evening time.

Chelsea Wine Bar `20 G8`
346 Lisburn Road
Phone (028) 9068 7177
Recently benefited from a facelift which can probably be said of one or two of its customers. When it first opened, the Chelsea was a standard bearer for the rejuvenation of the Lisburn Road, attracting a slightly older, well heeled crowd who tended to pack the place out most of the time. The opening of TaTu across the road took away a little bit of the gloss, but business remains brisk. The exterior won't win any awards for its architecture but inside is light and sunny throughout, especially upstairs, which has a conservatory feel to it. The drinks menu includes a list of thirty wines, a cocktail list and numerous draught and bottled beers, and an excellent range of food is served throughout the day and night. Popular late night haunt at weekends, with a tendency to attract thirty- and forty-somethings

in need of a good chablis to help them digest the terms of their divorce while they work on their chances of a rematch.

Cloth Ear `14 K11`
35-39 Waring Street
Phone (028) 9023 4888
Part of the sumptuous Merchant Hotel development, but with its own entrance, this is not just an enhancement to the Cathedral Quarter, it is among the most stylish bars in the city. The exterior is high Victorian, the interior modern by contrast, with lots of quirky touches from an array of 'Airfix' stags heads to the themed loos which are worth a visit even if nature isn't calling. Table footy. Currently the in place for Belfast's style conscious, but notoriously fickle, twenty- and thirtysomethings.

Crown Liquor Saloon `13 J10`
46 Great Victoria Street
Phone (028) 9027 9901
More has been written about this pub than any other in Belfast, and deservedly so. The Crown is such an architectural gem that it is in the care of the National Trust. The pub was built in 1849 but its opulent decor was created by Italian craftsmen who came to Belfast much later to work on the famous liners being built at Harland & Wolff shipyard. The result is an unrivalled example of a High Victorian Gin Palace with lots of stained glass, mosaic tiling and intricate wood carving. There are ten wooden snugs, somewhat reminiscent of old railway compartments, with some delightful attention to detail such as gas lighting and an original Victorian bell system for summoning service. More tourists visit this pub than any other in Belfast, but the clientele manages to remain fairly local. If you are visiting from outside Ireland and find yourself ordering your first ever pint of Guinness, you might as well go the whole hog and and try a bowl of

excellent Irish stew. You can even check the bar out via its own web-cam which can be accessed through the Belfast Telegraph web site at www.belfasttelegraph.co.uk.

Cutters Wharf `20 J6`
Lockview Rd
Phone (028) 9080 5100
Modern bar on the banks of the River Lagan and a welcome addition to fashionable Stranmillis, an area strangely devoid of pubs. One of only a few Belfast bars to offer fair weather drinkers the chance to sip something cool out of doors. The downstairs bar has scrapped the boat house look in favour of an eclectic mishmash while the River Grill upstairs has recently been revamped in an effort to broaden its appeal.

Deer's Head `13 J11`
1 Lower Garfield Street
Phone (028) 9023 9163
If you have just completed a lap or two of CastleCourt, or want to miss out on the event altogether, a stroll across the road will bring you to the Deer's Head where you can rest the soles of your feet in an attractive window snug while contemplating your next sortie over a quiet pint or a bite of lunch.

Duke of York `13 J11`
7-11 Commercial Court
Phone (028) 9024 1062
One of the oldest pubs in Belfast, the Duke of York is tucked up a cobbled side street in the Cathedral Quarter.. The pub has been totally refurbished but it retains its old world charm (the printing paraphernalia reflects its proximity to the city's former newspaper district). Live music several nights a week helps to pull the customers in after dark.

The Edge `14 L10`
Mays Meadows
Phone (028) 9032 2000
Riverside pub and restaurant which has struggled at times to reach 'full steam ahead' due in part to its slightly isolated location. Both the exterior and interior have their good points but, overall, the development has not lived up to its full potential. Everything is certainly on a grand scale, however, and the long stretch of riverside sun deck is certainly a crowd pleaser on a warm summers day.

The Eg `20 H7`
32-40 Malone Road
Phone (028) 9038 1994
Many bars in Belfast are spoken of in reference to another. So it is with the Eg and the Bot, two bars that stage a face off at the bottom end of the Malone Road, close to Queen's University. Both are among the busiest bars in town and each has been totally rebuilt in recent years. The Eg has abandoned its traditional roots and opted for a modern cafe bar look with back-lit racks of wine behind the bar, although beer remains the favourite tipple of the predominantly youthful clientele. Decent pub grub is on offer, and there's usually a DJ on hand to pump out some tunes.

The Empire `13 J9`
40-42 Botanic Avenue
Phone (028) 9032 8110
It was a long time in coming but it was the Empire that introduced live comedy to Belfast's pubs. Local boy made good, Paddy Kielty, used to compere the showcase of talent which comes from near and far every Tuesday night during term

Northern Whig on Bridge Street

time. Comedy upstairs in the Empire Music Hall, and a multitude of high quality musical events staged both upstairs and downstairs in the basement bar.

Errigle Inn `14 k9`
320 Ormeau Road
Phone (028) 9064 1410
An Ormeau Road stalwart which has enjoyed unbroken popularity for many years. A complex of bars, with a strong emphasis on live music and excellent bar food, which helps to give it more than just local appeal. The wood panelled, Oak Lounge allows you to lose track of day and night.

The Fly `13 J9`
5-6 Lower Crescent
Phone (028) 9050 9750
Located in an attractive Georgian crescent, the interior is dominated by a Gaudi-esque spiral staircase which winds its way through three bars. Recently refurbished, but a predominantly young crowd is still attracted by the old formula of music, dancing and drinks promotions.

Four Winds `27 M4`
111 Newton Park
Phone (028) 9070 7970

Top 5 Traditional Bars

The Crown
The Rotterdam
White's Tavern
The Morning Star
The Duke of York

Tuesday is stand-up comedy night at the Empire

Bar, wine bar and restaurant combo. A reputation for fine food makes it a popular alternative to city centre drinking.

The Front Page · 13 J12
110 Donegall Street
Phone (028) 9032 4924
So called due to its location in the heart of the city's newspaper district, the Front Page is a family owned bar best known for staging live music and club nights.

The Garrick · 14 K11
29 Chichester Street
Phone (028) 9032 1984
Recently renovated, the Front Bar has become the traditionally styled Public Bar where the absence of modern electronics is aimed at promoting the art of conversation. The adjacent Lounge Bar boasts an interesting array of artefacts, from Russian iconic art to a collection of barometers. Live music upstairs in The Room.

The Globe · 13 J9
36 University Road
Phone (028) 9050 9840
Has smartened up its image after undergoing its third change of identity in recent years, but remains a large bar near to Queen's University which caters to the local student population with a regular diet of musical events, including karaoke competitions for frustrated X Factor wannabes!

Irene & Nan's · 13 J10
12 Brunswick Street
Phone (028) 9023 9123
www.ireneandnans.com
Low lit, hip drinking space, with a very kitsch bar featuring an array of clocks that look like a series unwanted housewarming presents

John Hewitt in the Cathedral Quarter

dating back to the 1950's. Decent food and good cocktails. A bit quirky, but all the better for it.

The John Hewitt · 13 J12
51 Donegall Street
Phone (028) 9023 3768
Traditional style pub named after a local poet and located in the heart of the up and coming Cathedral Quarter. A combination of live music, traditional and jazz, and a growing reputation as a gastro pub has seen the John Hewitt establish a burgeoning clientele within a few years of it first opening its doors.

King's Head · 20 G8
829 Lisburn Road
Phone (028) 9050 9950
Situated on the edge of town, opposite the King's Hall, the King's Head has seen its popularity ebb and flow over the years but, following a recent refit, its star is firmly back in the ascendancy. This is one of the city's bigger pubs, with a separate entrance for the upstairs restaurant, a downstairs bar which is cleverly divided between a traditional pub space, and an area decked out in drawing room comfort. Customers include the young and old, and there's live music several times a week, performed in a separate conservatory area at the back.

The Kitchen · 14 K11
36-40 Victoria Square
Phone (028) 9032 4901
The Kitchen is dead - long live the Kitchen. The original Kitchen Bar had changed very little since it opened in 1859 but then came plans for Victoria Square, a £320m retail development, and a favourite watering hole was in the way. But like the proverbial phoenix, the pub has been sympathetically rebuilt nearby and the end result retains much of the old charm, right down to the preoccupation with football and horse racing. Even the famous Paddy Pizza with its soda bread base has survived the move.

Kremlin `13 J12`
96 Donegall Street
Phone (028) 9031 6061
www.kremlin-belfast.com
Some cities have a gay village, but Belfast made do for many years with a gay nightclub, albeit a very successful one. The city now has several gay bars and even its own Gay Pride festival at the end of July. You will spot the Kremlin by the statue of Lenin which stands over the door. The Russian theme continues inside with Tsar, the public bar, Long Bar, the disco bar, and Red Square, a split level nightclub area which stays open until three or four o'clock in the morning. The Kremlin has been going strong since 1999, and a recent expansion sees it set to remain gay HQ for some time to come.

La Lea `13 J10`
43 Franklin Street
Phone (028) 9023 0200
www.lalea.com
Stylish, late-night hangout above Bar Bacca, offering music and dancing until the wee small hours of the morning.

Lavery's Bar & Gin Palace
12-16 Bradbury Place `13 J9`
Phone (028) 9087 1106
At the risk of over-using the word, Lavery's really is a Belfast institution. Popular with students, but all forms of life are here to behold, often packed in like sardines. Don't be surprised if you step inside only to find that you're making your way along the bar without your feet touching the floor. A good spot to study life, but not so good if you are looking for a quiet drink. The first floor Bunker has live music seven days a week, and there are 19 pool tables on the top floor.

Katy Daly's, The Limelight, Spring and Airbrake
Ormeau Avenue `13 J10`
Phone (028) 9032 5942
Katy's is a traditional bar, best known for its association with the two live music venues either side of it. The Limelight has played host to a who's who of bands, including Oasis and the Strokes, while relative newcomer, Spring and Airbrake has already hosted James Blunt. Tuesday sees all three spaces given over to Belfast's favourite club night, Shag.

McCracken's Bar `14 K11`
4 Joy's Entry
Phone (028) 9032 6711
Formerly O'Neills, one of several city centre bars hidden up narrow alleyways, but this one is refreshingly modern. Relaxing lunchtime hideaway transforms into R 'n' B venue come Saturday night.

McHughs `14 K11`
29-31 Queen's Square
Phone (028) 9050 9990
The city's oldest surviving building, with parts of it dating back to 1711. When it was restored a few years ago, McHughs defied its slightly out of the way location and pulled in hordes of young professionals. Some have migrated to new watering holes that have sprung up in the meantime, but enough remain to keep the place busy most nights of the week. The layout consists of a ground floor bar, downstairs club

McHughs occupies Belfast's oldest building

Bar Bacca where Belfast meets Bangkok

and upstairs restaurant, all nicely designed on an open plan basis with a strong emphasis on exposed brickwork and quirky fittings. The most notable of these is a large chess set which is displayed in a glass cabinet at the back of the bar. The pieces have been modelled on various leading figures from Northern Ireland's over populated political world, and include such luminaries as Mo Mowlam, David Trimble, John Hulme, Gerry Adams and, of course, the big man himself, Ian Paisley.

The Merchant Hotel `14 K11`
35-39 Waring Street
Phone (028) 9023 4888
When Bill Clinton stayed in Belfast, the Europa was the best we had to offer. The fact that he opted to sleep in Dublin on his return to the city may, of course, have been coincidental. But now we have the Merchant, former Ulster Bank HQ and a must if you are looking to impress a business client, or a future wife, with a combination of sophisticated drinks menu and Georgian grandeur. If it's the future wife, you might be tempted to invest in the world's most expensive cocktail, a £750 Mai Tai. Alternatively, you might prefer to stick to a G&T in the hotel's intimate basement nightclub, **Ollie's,** where you can show

Spanish visitors enjoying a taste of the black stuff in the Crown Bar

her some of your best moves, safe in the knowledge that you have saved yourself the price of an engagement ring.

Milk
14 K12

10-14 Tomb Street
Phone (028) 9027 8876
www.clubmilk.com
Firmly established among the premier league of late night city clubbing. Crowds are drawn by big name DJ's, a striking interior and the promise of drinking and dancing

The Spaniard - Belfast's smallest pub?

late into the night.

mono
14 K11

96-100 Ann Street
Phone (028) 9027 8886
Bar cum club, which has recently undergone an expensive refit. The look is urban chic. The music is an eclectic mix of dance, house, and soul.

Morning Star
14 K11

17-19 Pottinger's Entry
Phone (028) 9032 3976
Salt of the earth, traditional pub, hidden down a narrow alleyway, right in the heart of the city's main shopping district. A listed building dating back to the early 18th century when it was a terminal for the Belfast to Dublin mail coach.

Morrison's
13 J10

21 Bedford Street
Phone (028) 9032 0030
Many preferred the Irish themed Spirit Grocer look, but the new contemporary image still draws the same crowd, including the odd local celebrity from the BBC across the road. Laid back cocktail lounge upstairs.

Mynt
14 K12

2-16 Dunbar Street
Phone (028) 9023 4520
Gay bar and nightclub. Formerly Parliament, then Kube, but remains a mainstay of the expanding gay scene in Belfast.

Northern Whig
13 J11

2-10 Bridge Street
Phone (028) 9050 9888
Long gone are the days when this imposing building was occupied by the Northern Whig printing presses. In the intervening years it seemed to sit rather forlornly in an unfashionable part of town, waiting for the good times to return. And now they have. Equal measures of vision and hard cash have transformed the interior into one of the most impressive eating and drinking spaces in the city. Many of the designer trappings are familiar, with the exception of a large pinch of communism in the shape of some old eastern bloc statues, but it is the grand scale of the original building which successfully brings the whole thing together. Popular place for lunch and still an 'in' place after dark, despite the growth in competition.

Odyssey Pavilion
14 L12

Queens Quay
The Odyssey complex includes a 10,000 seater arena, and a multiplex cinema, and the Odyssey Pavilion is designed to entertain audiences before and after the shows. The Pavilion has a couple of decent restaurants but when it comes to bars and clubs, the offering seems to be similar to what you get in the growing number of entertainment complexes sprouting up throughout the UK and Ireland. Themes are to the fore, and they include **Bambu Beach Club**, **Budda**, **Bar Seven** and **Precious.** Things can be a little quiet during the week, but the place livens up at weekends, attracting a mainly youthful crowd.

The Parlour `13 H9`
2-4 Elmwood Avenue
Phone (028) 9068 6970
Next door to Queen's Students' Union, and a favourite therefore with local undergraduates. What they don't spend on beer goes towards a tasty pizza from the bar's wood burning oven.

Potthouse `13 K11`
1 Hill Street
Phone (028)9024 4044
Site of Belfast's first pottery apparently, but looks more like a modern office block than a bar from the outside. Inside, by contrast, is a post industrial style bunker. Concrete, steel, glass and resin are the order of the day. Secure one of the half dozen curtained booths, sink into the sumptuous upholstery, and take root for the night. Alternatively, head upstairs to Sugar Room Nightclub, or blag your way onto the guest list for Soap Bar on the top floor. Glass floors. Hip place. One of the few bars in town with decent outdoor drinking space.

Pavilion Bar `14 K9`
296-298 Ormeau Road
Phone (028) 9028 3283
The Pavilion, which provides some local competition for the Errigle, comprises a large ground floor bar designed along traditional lines, an upstairs lounge, and a pool room on the top floor.

Queen's Cafe Bar `13 J11`
4 Queen's Arcade
Phone (028) 9032 1347
Attractive little bar tucked away up Queen's Arcade. Popular lunchtime stop for hungry shoppers, but stays busy on into the evening now that the city centre is becoming popular once again as a place to come drinking.

Robinson's `13 J10`
38-40 Great Victoria Street.
Phone (028) 9024 7447

Robinson's had long been a Belfast landmark when it was burnt to the ground several years ago. The rebuild has left it looking much as it did from the outside. On the inside, the front bar has been painstakingly restored in keeping with the Victorian original, but a multitude of themes feature throughout the other floors making it possible to do a pub crawl without actually leaving Robinsons. On top of all that, there's a wide variety of live music and club nights on offer.

Rotterdam Bar `14 K12`
52-54 Pilot Street
Phone (028) 9074 6021
It doesn't look like much from the outside, and you might well wonder why you went a bit out of your way to get here, but the Rotterdam is currently one of the most unspoilt traditional bars in Belfast. It occupies a fast changing world which has seen it recently surrounded by new office developments and apartment blocks along Clarendon Dock. Open the door though and you immediately step back in time. A roaring fire, low ceilings, bare brick walls and a tiled floor help to evoke a bygone era. Live music - traditional, pop, jazz & blues - is on offer most nights of the week and outdoor concerts on the dockside are a regular weekend feature during the summer months.

Ryan's Bar & Grill `20 G8`
116-118 Lisburn Road
Phone (028) 9050 9850
Modern take on a traditional bar,

> **Top 5 Style Bars**
>
> **TaTu**
> **Apartment**
> **Cloth Ear**
> **Irene & Nan's**
> **Northern Whig**

Modern architecture at TaTu

with quite a pleasing end result. This is a bar which rightly prides itself on serving good food, which is available all day until 11pm.

Skye `13 J10`
21 Howard Street
Phone (028) 9033 3313
You don't have to be old to remember the previous occupants of this site, the Washington, a popular student watering hole, followed by Shenanagan Rooms, which conformed to its Irish stereotyping by failing even to spell its own name correctly. The latest offering is pitched at young urbanites with an appetite for smart surroundings, loud music, dancing and cheap drink.

The Spaniard `14 K11`
3 Skipper Street
Phone (028) 9023 2448
Formerly Opium, but still a contender for smallest bar in Belfast. What it may lack in physical stature, it makes up for in personality. Dart board in tiny back room. Walls and ceiling decked out in record covers. Good music, and live gigs upstairs.

Three floors of cutting edge design at the Potthouse

over three floors. Popular gay venue with a busy diary of live entertainment, from bingo to to karaoke.

Vbar & M Club `13 J9`
23 Bradbury Place
Phone (028) 9023 3131
www.mclub.co.uk
Downstairs bar and upstairs nightclub where subtlety is not the watchword. Caters to a mainly young crowd with resident DJ's several nights a week. Tuesday and Thursday are student nights, while Friday is 70's night (that's the 1970's not the over 70's).

Wellington Park Hotel `20 H7`
21 Malone Road
Phone (028) 9038 1111
Before peace broke out, the Welly Park, as it is affectionately known, was an institution for Belfast twenty and thirtysomethings seeking late drink and romance, not necessarily in that order. Times have changed, things have moved on, new places have opened, and the Welly has mellowed somewhat. The foyer is so spacious that it is better stocked than an average branch of Sofaworld. There's even a grand piano to help promote the relaxed atmosphere which prevails during the week. Remains a popular weekend venue and guaranteed teenager free zone.

White's Tavern `13 J11`
1-4 Winecellar Entry
Phone (028) 9033 0988
Belfast city centre has a few pubs which are hidden away down narrow alleyways but the nice thing is that you feel you have unearthed a hidden jewel when you find them. White's fits firmly into this category. The stone floors, exposed brickwork, low beamed ceilings and the peat fire give credence to the fact that thirsts have been satisfied here since 1630.

Stiff Kitten `13 J10`
Bankmore Square
Phone (028) 9023 8700
Dance club established by the promoters of long established techno club night, Shine, at Queen's Students Union. Wide mix of resident and guest DJ's.

TaTu `20 G8`
701 Lisburn Road
Phone (028) 9038 0818
In the same way that the Crown stands head and shoulders above some very good traditional bars in Belfast, so TaTu reigns supreme when it comes to the city's style bars, despite the fact that it lies a mile or two out of town at the southern end of the Lisburn Road. A former snooker hall, this is a project which proves what a good architect and a creative imagination can achieve. The interior design has been tweaked recently but the overall look continues to ooze style and sophistication, right down to the smallest detail. It's hardly surprising that TaTu manages to attract a swarm of designer thirty-somethings who come to enjoy the sights

and sounds of the bar, and the good food served by the restaurant. All in all, a bar that would grace any city in the world.

Ten Square `13 J10`
10 Donegall Square South
Phone (028) 9024 1001
Trendy boutique hotel. After a false start, the layout has been revamped into Grill Room & Bar, and with great success. Buzzing with smartly dressed drinkers and diners, enjoying professional service in attractive surroundings.

Thompson's `13 J11`
3 Patterson's Place
Phone (028) 9032 3762
Situated down a quiet side street close to the City Hall, this is one of the city's leading late night clubbing venues, with well established events such as Funkarama every Wednesday.

Union Street `13 J12`
8-14 Union Street
Phone (028) 9031 6060
Converted 19th century shoe factory laid out as a bar and restaurant

Belfast has hundreds of restaurants and cafés to choose from but this guide attempts to select about 50 of the best. This process is bound to be subjective but no apologies are made for that. After all, how many times have you eaten at a restaurant for the first time because it happened to be recommended to you by somebody else?

All establishments featured have been tried out, often frequently, by somebody connected with the Belfast Street Atlas & Guide. They have been selected by people who enjoy good food and drink, bearing in mind price, location and diversity. This Guide does not accept advertising and so these places are simply the ones that we have enjoyed most - the ones that we recommend to friends and relatives. They don't always agree, and perhaps you won't either, but that's what being subjective is all about! Having said that, we would be keen to hear your own recommendations or any objections that you might have regarding any of our choices.

What can be said, without fear of contradiction, is that the restaurant scene in Belfast has been transformed over the past ten years. Choice and quality have improved tremendously, and this trend looks set to continue. In terms of culinary diversity, price and atmosphere, Belfast restaurants can hold their own against most UK and Irish cities.

Many are mentioned in the growing array of good food guides. These publications all have their good points but, invariably, one area of contention is their attempts to estimate the likely cost of a meal. We have all had the experience of going somewhere supposedly "cheap & cheerful" only to find that a couple of drinks and a shared bottle of wine can do strange things to the bill. On the other hand, there are occasions when you may have taken advantage of a very reasonable fixed price menu, and left with both your conscience and the contents of your wallet largely intact! When you add in lunchtime and early evening specials, fixed-price menus and happy hours, attempts to estimate

Price Rating	
£	Cheap (usually under £15 per head)
££	Moderate (between £15 and £30)
£££	Expensive (£30+)

price often tend to be in vain. The system adopted for this guide, therefore, is rather broad-brush in its approach, attempting to categorise a restaurant as expensive, moderate or cheap.

"Expensive" restaurants are those where you can expect the final bill to exceed £30 per head. If you eat somewhere categorised as "cheap", you will often escape for less than a tenner. The final bill at a restaurant falling into the moderate category should fall somewhere between £15 and £30, bearing in mind all the caveats mentioned earlier.

Finally, the golden rule when using this guide is to phone first! The restaurant trade is a fast changing world with around 40% of the entries below appearing on our pages for the first time. We have tried to be as accurate as we can be at the time of writing, but restaurants come and go, change ownership, chefs, menus, opening hours and much else, so it is best to check with the restaurant before turning up.

Alden's   `15 Q10`

229 Upper Newtownards Road
Phone (028) 9065 0079
www.aldensrestaurant.com
Price Rating: £££
From the moment you are greeted as you come through the door at Alden's, there is great attention to detail. Service which is friendly but discreet, a nicely appointed dining room with plenty of space between the tables, and classic brasserie food which reaches exacting standards. Alden's is located in the east of the city, and it might not enjoy the cachet

of one or two of its more centrally located rivals, but it remains in the upper reaches of Belfast's premier league of restaurants. Great value business lunch is served Monday to Friday. *Open: Mon-Fri 12noon-2.30pm & 6pm-10pm; Sat 6pm-11pm*

Alto's   `13 J11`

6 Fountain Street
Phone (028) 9032 3087
Price Rating: £
Of the many cafes on Fountain Street this is our favourite, although the effort to impress is reflected in the price. The high ceilinged dining room is cool and airy, as is the soundtrack, and the walls are lined with modern art. The menu doesn't stay the same for long but it's normally innovative and tends to have a strong Mediterranean accent. An extensive selection of Italian wines and a few outside tables are an added bonus. *Opening Times: Mon-Sat 10am-6pm (until 8pm Thurs)*

Beatrice Kennedy   `14 K12`

44 University Road
Phone (028) 9020 2290
Price Rating: ££
www.beatricekennedy.co.uk
Intimate restaurant named after the lady who used to live here before it became an eaterie. The dining room retains much of the period feel of the house and the menu tends to stick to solid and dependable favourites which keep the customers coming back for more. Nice place to treat your great aunt to Sunday lunch, in the hope that your investment will be returned manifold as a result! Popular choice for pre-theatre dining. *Opening Times: Mon-Sat 5pm-10.15pm; Sunday 12.30pm-2.30pm & 5pm-8.15pm*

Bengal Brasserie   `14 K9`

455 Ormeau Road
Phone (028) 9064 7516
Price Rating: ££
Recently moved along the road to the former premises of Dish. A local favourite but worth going out of your way for the intimate setting and the ever evolving menu.

2Taps brings a little bit of Spain to the Cathedral Quarter

Bennett's on Belmont `15 Q11`
4 Belmont Road
Phone (028) 9065 6590
Price Rating: £

With the honourable exception of Alden's, east Belfast is not spoiled for choice when it comes to eating out. No surprise then that recent arrival, Bennett's, received a warm welcome from day one for its designer interior, friendly staff, and interesting food at affordable prices. Every neighbourhood should have a local diner as good as this. *Open daily 9am-9pm.*

The Big Easy `13 J10`
34-36 Bedford Street
Phone (028) 9031 1026
Price Rating: ££

More reincarnations than Doctor Who. Formerly Larry's, then Reno's, now the Big Easy, a New Orleans themed eaterie with a relaxed air and regular live jazz and blues. *Opening Times: Mon-Sat 11.30am-1am*

Bishops `13 J9`
30 Bradbury Place
Phone (028) 9043 9070
Price Rating: £

Decent fish and chips served almost 24/7 in commendably smart and comfy setting. Other branches on Botanic Avenue and Stranmillis Road *Opening Times: Mon-Sun 10am-2am*

Cafe Paul Rankin
27-29 Fountain Street `13 J11`
Phone (028) 9031 5090
43 Arthur Street `13 J11`
Phone (028) 9031 0108
601-605 Lisburn Road `20 G8`
Phone (028) 9066 8350
www.rankingroup.co.uk
Price Rating: £

The look and feel of the two city centre outlets are similar - foot-sore shoppers and office workers, enjoying modern, simple cooking which utilises only the best, fresh ingredients. Good coffee, delicious patisserie, outdoor seating when the weather permits, and a take away service if you haven't got time to linger. *Opening Times: Mon-Sat 7.30am-6pm (until 9pm on Thurs)*

Cafe Renoir `13 J9`
95 Botanic Avenue
Phone (028) 9031 1300
www.cafe-renoir.com
Price Rating: £

---

5 For Business

Nick's Warehouse
Alden's
Restaurant Michael Deane
Roscoff Brasserie
James Street South

The original outlet on Queen Street is still as popular as ever with lunchtime shoppers and office workers, but Renoir has pulled off a masterstroke with the opening of a new cafe, bistro and pizzeria combo on Botanic Avenue. Busy from breakfast through to lunch and dinner, with punters enjoying an interesting array of burgers, noodles and pasta dishes. The pizzas are not the cheapest in town, but they are among the best. Join the throng. *Opening Times: Mon-Sat 8am-10.30pm; Sun 9am-10.30pm.*

Caffe Casa
1 James Street South `13 J10`
Phone 9031 9970
12-14 College Street `13 J11`
Phone (028) 9031 9900
price Rating: £

Great stop for coffee or a quick bite of lunch. Homemade soup and bread, gourmet sarnies, baguettes and wraps. Plenty of seating, but take away service available if you don't have time to rest your weary bones.

Cargoes `20 G8`
613 Lisburn Road
Phone (028) 9066 5451
Price Rating: £

Long established cafe and delicatessen serving morning coffee, lunch and afternoon tea from a menu which changes on a daily basis, but always includes a good choice of salads, salami and cheeses. *Opening Times: Mon-Sat 9.30am-5pm*

Cayenne `13 J9`
Shaftesbury Square
Phone (028) 9033 1532
www.rankingroup.co.uk
Price Rating: £££

They say that you can't judge a book by its cover. The same certainly applies to the excellent Cayenne and its uninspiring exterior which suggests that you should be dropping off your dry cleaning. Roscoff, Paul and Jeanne Rankin's initial venture at this location in 1989 was the first in Northern Ireland to be awarded a Michelin Star. When the star went east, it was decided to opt for a more informal, mid-market approach, and

Cayenne was born in 1999. The interior has expanded but remains modernist and slightly quirky, and the extra capacity is invariably filled due to cutting edge cooking which is is among the very best in Ireland. *Opening Times: Mon-Fri 12noon-2.15pm; Mon-Thurs 6pm-10.15pm; Fri-Sat 6pm-11.15pm; Sun 5pm-8.45pm.*

Clements

66-68 Botanic Avenue `13 J9`
4 Donegall Square West `13 J11`
131-133 Royal Avenue `13 J11`
139 Stranmillis Road `20 J7`
37-39 Rosemary Street `13 J11`
342 Lisburn Road `20 G8`
Price Rating: £
The Irish, apparently, drink more cups of tea per head than anybody else in the world. So why the current love affair with coffee? Perhaps the answer lies in where we are drinking it these days. A dependable cup of tea at home, but something more exotic as soon as our heads are turned by one of a new multitude of designer coffee houses to spring up around town. Clements is a case in point, and the Botanic Avenue outlet is a prime example. Soft leather sofas, funky decor with trademark rainbow-coloured light boxes, newspapers & magazines, music, hustle & bustle, more coffee choices than you could shake a stick at, and some very good sandwiches, wraps and tasty morsels to satisfy a sweet tooth (blueberry and white chocolate scone comes highly recommended). Who said you can't beat a nice cup of tea?

Conor `20 J7`

11a Stranmillis Road
Phone (028) 9066 3266
Price Rating: £
Situated across the road from the Ulster Museum and Botanic Gardens. Popular stop for coffee and elevenses. Decent bistro food served at lunch and dinner, but the highlight is the room which previously served as studio to the famous Belfast artist, William Conor. The space is bathed in natural light which pours through a glass vaulted ceiling, allowing diners

to appreciate the artwork which lines the walls, including a portrait of the man himself.

Deane's Brasserie `13 J10`

38-40 Howard Street
Phone (028) 9033 1134
www.michaeldeane.co.uk
Price Rating: ££
Restaurant Michael Deane, upstairs, holds the only Michelin Star in Belfast, but the downstairs brasserie is more mainstream and informal, concentrating on fresh local ingredients delivered with imagination. The interior has never lived up to the food, however, and the opening of the fresh and modern Deane's Deli just around the corner may see some regulars voting with their feet. *Opening Times: Mon-Sat 12noon-3pm & 5.30pm-10pm (until 11pm Fri & Sat)*

Deane's Deli `13 J10`

42-44 Bedford Street
Phone (028) 9024 8800
www.michaeldeane.co.uk
Price Rating: ££
New restaurant and deli combo which has proved to be an instant hit. Nothing too complicated about the menu, daily specials on the blackboard, a laid back atmosphere, and even the chance to spot a familiar face or two 'off telly' as it seems to be a popular alternative to the BBC canteen. *Opening Times: Mon-Sat 11.30am-10pm. Deli store open from 8am*

Dim Sum Restaurant `13 J9`

82 Botanic Avenue
Phone (028) 9043 9590
Price Rating: ££
The overall standard of Belfast's food

Flour - hip, cool and change from a fiver

Beatrice Kennedy on University Rd

scene continues to rise, but no sector enjoys strength in depth to match the city's Chinese restaurants. The Sun Kee has flown the flag for many years, followed more recently by the Red Panda, the Water Margin and Macau. Dim Sum (formerly Tong Dynasty) is firmly ensconced in the heavyweight division. In the same way that nervous flyers need only check for a look of panic on the faces of their cabin crew, authentic Chinese cuisine can usually be distinguished by the presence of Chinese diners, and Dim Sum certainly scores highly on this count. *Opening Times: Mon-Thurs 12noon-10pm; Fri-Sat 12noon-12midnight; Sun 11am-10pm*

Doorsteps `20 G8`

455-457 Lisburn Road
Phone (028) 9068 1645
Price Rating: £
Anywhere with a queue out the door at lunchtime warrants a mention. Cafe and gourmet sandwich shop with a selection of more than 70 sandwiches to choose from.

Equinox `13 J10`

32 Howard Street
Phone (028) 9023 0089
Price Rating: £
Recently extended Equinox is best known as a shop where discerning brides leave their wedding list so that they can stock up on Alessi, and other such brands of kitchen and dinner

Deane's Deli has been an instant hit

ware, at somebody else's expense! The small cafe area at the back is an additional treat where you can select from a goat's cheese and olive type menu and dine off a Rosenthal plate. If you are a student of time and motion, the ability to merge coffee, lunch, and designer shopping into one seamless action is bound to be a satisfying experience. *Opening Times: Mon-Sat 9.30am-4.45pm.*

Flour Crepe Room 46 `13 J11`
46 Upper Queen Street
Phone (028) 9033 9966
Price Rating: £
If you feel that the words 'hip', 'cool' and 'crepe' are unlikely bedfellows, you haven't been to Flour. The staff appear to be fans of Men in Black, the crepes are made while you wait, to eat in (just three tables) or to take away. The combinations are exhaustive, from 'bacon, egg, mushroom & cheese' to Mars Bar & Baileys Cream', and there's a range of tea, coffee and juice to wash them down. All that, and change from a fiver! *Opening Times: Mon-Sat 7.30am-5.30pm (until 8.30p Thurs).*

Ginger `13 J10`
7-8 Hope Street
Phone (028) 9024 4421
Price Rating: ££
Having established a glowing reputation on the Ormeau Road, Ginger has headed into the centre of town and goes from strength to strength. Intimate room and inspired bistro cooking. *Opening Times: Mon-Sat 12noon-3pm & 5pm-10pm*

Gingeroot `13 J10`
75 Great Victoria Street
Phone (028) 9031 3124
www.gingeroot.com
Price Rating: ££
North Indian cuisine, with an emphasis on spicy, tandoori-cooked dishes, served up in a modern setting to the accompaniment of Bollywood movies. *Opening Times: Mon-Sat 12noon-3pm & 5.30pm-11.30pm; Sun 5pm-10.30pm*

Ginger Tree `13 J9`
23 Donegall Pass
phone (028) 9032 7151
Price Rating: ££
Northern Ireland's flagship for Japanese dining has relocated from Ballyclare to the centre of town and now enjoys a view of a fortified police station. Fortunately the authentic food and serene service more than make up for the lacklustre setting. *Opening Times: Mon-Sun 12.30pm-2.30pm & 5pm-9.30pm*

Giraffe `20 J7`
54-56 Stranmillis Road
Phone (028) 9050 9820
Price Rating: £
OK, it's been a hard day at work, you're hungry, but you don't fancy being confronted by a naked chef in Sainsbury's, and there's very little apart from alcohol in the fridge. The answer is to grab the booze and head for Giraffe. The menu concentrates on the familiar: lots of pizza, pasta, meat & fish, with a few variations on the theme from the specials board. But it's all good tucker and there's usually a welcoming buzz about the place. And when it comes to paying the bill, you'll have your fridge to thank for the damage limitation. Open daily from 8am for breakfast, lunch and dinner.

Harbour View `14 K11`
1 Lanyon Quay
Phone (028) 9023 8823
www.harbourviewbelfast.co.uk
Price Rating: £££
Big budget riverside restaurant specialising in Japanese Teppanyaki dining, a sizzling, up close and personal experience where your food is prepared and cooked at your table. *Opening Times: Mon-Sun 12noon-11pm*

Istana Malaysian Restaurant
127 Great Victoria Street `13 J10`
Phone (028) 9032 2311
Price rating: ££
Authentic Malay cooking which reflects Chinese, Thai and Indian influences. *Opening Times: Mon-Fri 12noon-2.30pm & 5pm-11,30pm; Sat-Sun 5pm-11.30pm*

James Street South `13 J10`
21 James Street South
Phone (028) 9043 4310
www.jamesstreetsouth.co.uk
Price Rating: £££
A restaurant that takes itself seriously, from the tasteful warehouse conversion, to the professional service and the ultra modern cooking which many people consider to be the best in town. Would not look out of place in the City of London. The lunch and pre-theatre menus offer good value. *Open: Mon-Sat 12-2.45pm & 5.45pm-10.34pm; Sun 5.30pm-9pm.*

Jharna Tandoori `20 G8`
133 Lisburn Road
Phone (028) 9038 1299
Price Rating: ££
Traditional Indian restaurant with a good reputation built up over many years. *Open: Mon-Sat 12noon-2pm & 5.30pm-11.30pm; Sun 5.30pm-11pm.*

---

5 For Wooing

Cayenne
Ginger
Deanes Deli
Shu
Ten Square Grill Bar

Macau `14 K9`

271 Ormeau Road
Phone (028) 9069 1800
Price Rating: ££
One of the hottest tables in town due to a combination of limited space, great service, keen prices, a bring your own booze policy, but primarily the fact that the Chinese food is sublime. Book again on your way out. *Opening Times: Tues-Sun 5.30pm-11pm*

Maggie Mays `13 J9`

50 Botanic Avenue
Phone (028)9032 2662
Price Rating: £
You tried your first half of Guinness last night, and ended up consuming the full gallon. Fear not, the antidote is at hand in the shape of an Ulster fry. Even if you didn't make it out of bed until afternoon, you're still in luck at Maggie May's diner where the all day breakfast will work its magic. Wide range of tasty, homemade alternatives available, including veggie options. Unlicensed but can bring your own bottle. *Opening Times: Mon-Sun 9am-11pm*

Merchant Hotel `14 K11`

35-39 Waring Street
Phone (028) 9023 4888
www.themerchanthotel.com
Price Rating: £££
The former banking hall at 19th century Ultser Bank HQ is now the **Great Room Restaurant** at Belfast's leading boutique hotel, and by far the grandest dining room in Belfast. The classical cooking is in keeping with the room, but the sheer grandeur of the setting can make for a slightly rarefied atmosphere. *Open daily for breakfast, lunch, afternoon tea and dinner*

Molly's Yard `20 J9`

1 College Green Mews
Phone (028) 9032 2600
New bistro cum micro brewery venture housed in a converted stable block just off Botanic Avenue. There's nothing else quite like it, and it has been busy from day one. A few outdoor tables, small downstairs bar,

Molly's Yard - stable block turned bistro cum micro brewery

with the main dining space in the light and airy former hayloft. *Opening Times Mon-Sat 11am-9.30pm*

Mourne Seafood Bar `13 J11`

34-36 Bank Street
Phone (028) 9024 8544
www.mourneseafoodbar.com
Price Rating: ££
Next door to Kelly's Cellars may not be the first place you would think of setting up a new restaurant venture, but the sheer quality of the place is sure to guarantee success despite the hideaway location. Pleasant two storey interior - lots of bare wood and exposed brick - but it's the freshness of the locally sourced ingredients, the simplicity of the cooking, the friendly service and keen prices which will ensure that customers return for more. A breath of fresh sea air. *Opening Times: Mon-Tues 12noon-6pm; Wed-Thur 12noon-9.30pm; Fri-Sat 12noon-10.30pm; Sun 1pm-6pm*

Nick's Warehouse `14 K12`

35-39 Hill Street
Phone (028) 9043 9690
www.nickswarehouse.co.uk
Price Rating: ££
Restaurant and wine bar situated in what used to be a rather unfashionable part of town near to St Anne's Cathedral. Nick's pioneering spirit has been rewarded with a large and loyal following, especially among the business community who help to guarantee its enduring popularity both at lunchtime and in the evening. The Anix, a recent extension of the downstairs wine bar into the building next door, has added much needed capacity but there's still a good buzz throughout. The menu is constantly evolving, but the food is invariably cooked with zest, and the staff are exceptionally helpful if you require a second opinion on anything. *Opening Times: Mon-Fri 12noon-3pm; Tues-Sat 6pm-9.30pm*

Nick's - flagship of the Cathedral Quarter

Speranza - one of the early pioneers of Italian food in Belfast

young and old, business and casual, enjoy good, uncomplicated food and excellent service, from breakfast through to dinner.

Olive Tree Co `14 K9`
353 Ormeau Road
Phone (028) 9064 8898
Price Rating: £
Chilled out cafe cum delicatessen where you can enjoy rustic French cooking at lunchtime before stocking up on stuffed olives and foie gras to take the sad look off your fridge when you get home.

Pizza Express
25-27 Dublin Road `13 J10`
Phone (028) 9032 9050
551 Lisburn Road `20 G8`
Phone (028) 9068 7700
Price Rating: £
Long established UK chain whose enduring success relies upon prime locations, stylish, open-plan interiors, friendly service, and arguably the best pizzas in town, although alternatives are limited to a couple of pasta dishes and a couple of salads. A no booking policy is the norm except for large groups. *Opening Times: Mon-Sun 11.30am-11pm*

Printers Wine Bar `13 J12`
33 Lower Donegall Street
Phone (028) 9031 3404
Price Rating: £
Recent addition to the Cathedral Quarter, with its entrance tucked away on Commercial Court, opposite

Duke of York. Long, narrow room, nicely appointed, and already a popular pit stop for lunchtime tapas. *Opening Times: Mon-Wed 8.30am-3pm; Thurs-Fri 8.30am-9.30pm*

Pulp `13 J10`
52 Howard Street
Phone (028) 9032 6650
Belfast's first juice bar. Why not mainline a week's worth of vitamin C, and treat yourself to a delicious bagel while you're at it. *Opening Times: Mon-Fri 7am-4.30pm*

Rain City `20 H7`
33-35 Malone Road
Phone (028) 9068 2929
www.rankingroup.co.uk
Price Rating: ££
Part of the ever expanding Rankin empire, this time going for the look and feel of a west coast American diner. A good cross section of diners,

---

5 For The Craic

2Taps
Scalini
Zen
Molly's Yard
Villa Italia

Red Panda
60 Great Victoria Street `13 J10`
Phone (028) 9080 8700
Odyssey Pavilion, Queens Qy `14 K11`
Phone (028) 9046 6644
www.theredpanda.co.uk
Price Rating: ££
Authentic Hong Kong Chinese cuisine served in a large modern layout just across the road from the Europa Hotel. Both outlets are relatively new, but are usually busy trying to satisfy Belfast's seemingly insatiable appetite for Chinese food. Good value business lunch. Open daily for lunch and dinner (except for Sat lunch).

Restaurant Michael Deane `13 J10`
36 Howard Street
Phone (028) 9033 1134
www.michaeldeane,co.uk
Price Rating: £££+
If you are looking for somewhere informal to let your hair down, this is not it. Michael Deane currently holds the only Michelin Star in Northern Ireland, and he is meticulously old school when it comes to classic *haute cuisine*. The service matches the formality of the food. For serious foodies. *Opening Times: Wednesday-Saturday 7pm-9.30pm*

Revelations Internet Cafe `13 J9`
27 Shaftesbury Square
Phone (028) 9032 0337
Belfast's first internet cafe. If you are addicted to caffeine and email, pop in and satisfy two cravings, albeit not for the price of one. £4 per hour for web access. *Opening Times: Mon-Fri 10am-10pm; sat 10am-6pm; Sun 11am-7pm*

Roscoff Brasserie `13 J10`
7-11 Linenhall Street
Phone (028) 9031 1150
www.rankingroup.co.uk
Price Rating: £££
The Rankin name is ubiquitous when it comes to TV cookery shows and

dining out in Belfast. It was surprising, therefore, that Roscoff, the name of their maiden venture in Belfast, and the first recipient of a Michelin star in Northern Ireland, disappeared from the culinary lexicon when the restaurant changed tack and was renamed, Cayenne. But now, after an absence of five years, Roscoff is back, taking up residence in an impressive room which used to be home to Christies Brasserie. This is high end dining, classic French cooking, lots of business suits at lunchtime, and special occasion diners in the evening. *Opening Times: Mon-Fri 12noon-2.15pm & 6pm-10.15pm; Sat 6pm-11.15pm*

Scalini   `13 J9`
85 Botanic Avenue
Phone (028) 9032 0303
www.scalinirestaurant.co.uk
Price Rating: ££
Scalini is Italian for steps, a name which is appropriate for a 250 seater restaurant spread over 4 levels. Belfast has several excellent Italian restaurants which are big on lively atmosphere, but not too demanding when it comes to paying. This is another. Extensive menu, very reasonable prices, and a striking decor. A friendly, family restaurant which is well worth a visit. No booking unless you are a group of 8 or more. *Opening Times: Mon-Sat 5pm-11pm; Sun 4pm-10.30pm.*

Shu   `20 G8`
253 Lisburn Road
Phone (028) 9038 1655
www.shu-restaurant.com
Price Rating: £££
Times have changed since this was the Terrace Restaurant. The layout is basically the same, but the old basement wine bar has been replaced with a trendy cocktail and tapas bar while the main dining area at ground level has also had a complete makeover which gives it a rather up-market feel - modern, yet sumptuous, with lashings of dark wood, leather upholstery and designer fittings. The menu concentrates on top quality bistro clas-

sics, and attentive service helps to ensure an enjoyable meal. A good place to impress a prospective partner, regardless of whether your intentions are business or pleasure. *Open: Mon-Sat 12noon-2.30pm & 6pm-10pm.*

Speranza   `13 J9`
16-19 Shaftesbury Square
Phone (028) 9023 0213
Price Rating: ££
Under new ownership, but still a local Italian albeit with a few extras on the menu. If a restaurant continues to flourish more than twenty years after it first opened, it must be doing many things right. Speranza is such a place, and part of the reason for its success is that it has never stood still for long, nor taken its customers for granted. A recent refit using acres of glass and steel gives it a cutting edge look, but at heart it is still a warm and friendly Italian eaterie, offering a menu which concentrates primarily on pizzas and pasta. The atmosphere is lively and informal and children are made welcome. *Opening Times: Mon-Sat 5.30pm-11.30pm; Sun 5.30pm-10.30pm.*

The Sun Kee   `13 J9`
43-47 Donegall Pass
Phone (028) 9031 2016
Price Rating: ££
In the name of progress, the Sun Kee has crossed the road to premises formerly occupied by the Manor House, but many will miss feeling that they had unearthed a gem when emerging from the humble surroundings that used to call home. Some things have not changed, however. The food continues to be among the best and most authentic Chinese cuisine available

Follow the queue to Villa Italia

Ginger's new pad in the city

anywhere in the country. *Opening Times: Mon-Sun 12noon-11pm*

Suwanna   `13 J10`
117 Great Victoria Street
Phone (028) 9043 9007
Price Rating: ££
Not that enticing from the outside but, in the opinion of many, the best Thai food in Belfast is served attentively within. *Opening Times: Mon-Sat 6pm-10.30pm*

Swanton's Gourmet Foods
639 Lisburn Road   `20 G8`
Phone (028) 9068 3388
Price Rating: £
Attractive cafe cum deli catering to a loyal lunchtime following among the ladies of south Belfast.

Taps & 2Taps
479-481 Lisburn Road   `20 G8`
Phone (028) 9066 3211
30 Waring Street   `14 K11`
Phone (028) 9031 1414
Price Rating: £
Belfast is rarely associated with sun, sand and sangria, but locals took to tapas like ducks to water from the first day sleek and trendy Taps Wine Bar arrived on the Lisburn Road. Initial success has been followed up with the opening of 2Taps opposite the Merchant Hotel in the now thriving Cathedral Quarter. Chorizo, gambas and tortilla remain the order of the

Zen - Japanese food & designer interior

day, but there is an attractive area for outdoor dining, and the fact that it is next door to the Potthouse means that there is usually a healthy quota of eye candy who have adopted it as pre-clubbing restaurant of choice. *Taps open: Mon-Thurs 12noon-2.30pm & 5pm-10pm; Fri & Sat 12noon-11pm. 2Taps open: Mon 12noon-3pm; Tues-Sat 12noon-1am*

Tedford's `14 K11`
5 Donegall Quay
Phone (028) 9043 4000
Price Rating: £££
Fish restaurant occupying a former ship chandlers on the banks of the Lagan overlooking the weir. The choice of fish is extensive although a little bit expensive, but the end product is invariably fresh and beautifully prepared. Meat lovers are catered for also. Intimate space, but those who are tired of looking at their other half should note that tables upstairs come with a view of the river. *Opening Times: Tues-Fri 12noon-2.30pm; Tues-Sat 5pm-10pm.*

Ten Square Grill Room `13 J10`
10 Donegall Square South
Phone (028) 9024 1001
www.tensquare.co.uk
Price Rating: ££
Revamped layout has created a bar cum brasserie space that is chilled out during the day but buzzing with a smartly dressed, cocktail sipping crowd by night. Simple food, well executed. *Food served daily from breakfast until 10pm*

Thai-tanic Noodle Bar `20 H8`
2 Eglantine Avenue
Phone (028) 9066 8811
Price Rating: £
Okay, it is a very dodgy pun, and the place is hardly more than a takeaway, but there's a table and bench seating for 8 lucky punters to enjoy authentic Thai cooking for a fiver. *Opening Times: Tues-Fri 12noon-2.30pm & 5pm-11pm; Sat-Sun 5pm-11pm.*

Villa Italia `13 J9`
37-41 University Road
Phone (028) 9032 8356
www.villaitaliarestaurant.co.uk
Price Rating: ££
Despite having 300 seats, Villa Italia has taught Belfast quite a bit about the art of queuing over the past twenty years, but its popularity remains undimmed despite a no-booking policy (except for groups of 8 or more) and increasing competition from new outlets nearby. Its success is based on a formula of reasonably priced Italian food served by personable staff in one of the liveliest spots in town. *Open: Mon-Fri 5pm-11.30pm; Sat 4pm-11.30pm; Sun 4pm-10.30pm.*

The Water Margin `13 J9`
159-161 Donegall Pass
Phone (028) 9032 6888
Price Rating: ££
There is nothing understated about the Water Margin. Spread over two floors of a converted church, the decor is outlandish, and the menu so exhaustive that it should be printed in hard-

A breath of fresh sea air at Mourne

back. A winning combination of imaginative setting, efficient service, and religiously good Chinese food. *Opening Times: Mon-Sun 12noon-11pm*

Welcome Chinese Restaurant
22 Stranmillis Road `20 J7`
Phone (028) 9038 1359
www.welcome-group.co.uk
Price Rating : ££
For more than thirty years the Welcome has acted as a benchmark for many others that have come and gone. A recent refurbishment and extension indicates that there is plenty of time left to enjoy the highly rated cooking which is a combination of Cantonese, Pekinese and Szechwan. The choice of dishes is extensive. *Opening Times: Mon-Fri 12noon-2.15pm & 5pm-10.45pm; Sat 5pm-11.15pm; Sun 5pm-10.15pm*

Zen `13 J10`
55-59 Adelaide Street
Phone (028) 9023 2244
Price Rating: £££
Belfast has hardly been in the vanguard when it comes to the rise in the popularity of Japanese cuisine in the UK in recent years. Zen offers a menu which aims to rectify that situation, although purists might argue that it lacks authenticity, as the place is run mainly by Chinese staff. But Belfast does things its own way, and what you get here is a fabulously appointed restaurant, covering two floors, catering to 150 diners and, when the saki gets flowing, it is undoubtedly one of the hottest restaurants in the city. *Opening Times: Mon-Fri 12noon-3pm & 5pm-11pm; Sat 6pm-11.30pm; Sun 1.30pm-10.30pm*

Zio `13 J9`
23 University Road
Phone (028) 9027 8788
www.ziocafebar.com
Price Rating: ££
Busy Italian, part of an expanding chain across Northern Ireland, offering wide choice of pizza, pasta, meat and fish at prices that won't break the bank. *Opening Times: Mon-Sun 12noon-10pm*